og Kærlig
Kyss og hilsen
Marybeth

Painted Rooms

This book is dedicated to my wife, Ingebjørg
who has been standing beside me, supporting me
and helping me in my work throughout the years.

Painted Rooms

Scandinavian Interiors by Sigmund Aarseth

Text and photographs by Gudmund Aarseth

First published in the USA in 2004
Copyright © 2004 by Gudmund Aarseth

Photography, text, typesetting
and design by Gudmund Aarseth

Edited by Diane Edwards

Japanese translation by Tokiko Shima

Printed and bound in Greeley, Colorado
by the Kendall Printing Company

ISBN 0-9674583-5-8

Distributed in the USA by
Nordic Arts
3208 Snowbrush Place,
Fort Collins, CO 80521
Fax (970) 229-5683
Email: Diaedwards@cs.com

CONTENTS

THE NORWEGIAN HOME

Appearances can be deceptive in Norway. From the outside houses are often low-key and conservative in the use of color, typically painted either red or white. However, behind the doors of the most anonymous looking and modestly sized farmhouse you pass on the way there may be hidden gems that remain unknown to passers-by.

Norway has few majestic palaces, grand cathedrals and imposing manors. What Norwegian buildings might lack in scale however, is often compensated for by stunning natural surroundings that would put the largest of man-made constructions in the shade.

Since Norway is a relatively small country on the northernmost fringes of Europe, it has traditionally had a less urban culture than its neighbors Sweden and Denmark. Norway has always been open to foreign influences, although such cultural imports have been merged with a strong sense of national pride and tradition.

The wooden house
In a country where vast areas are covered by pine forests, it comes as no surprise that wood has always been the building material of choice. Log houses have been built in Norway since medieval times. They must surely rank among the simplest wood constructions imaginable, since they use more or less untreated logs in their construction. As industrial saw mills made

prepared wooden planks and paneling cheaper and more available, many such log houses were clad in wood paneling both inside and out. Gradually, wood frame constructions came to dominate since they required fewer raw materials and allowed for generous quantities of insulation.

In urban areas wooden houses had their distinct disadvantages — virtually all Norwegian cities and towns, originally made up of wooden houses, have at some point in their history been ravaged by devastating fires and rebuilt in brick or stone.

Traditional log houses renovated by Sigmund Aarseth.

Painted Rooms

The painted interior is typical for Norway and Sweden. Continental domestic interiors may have been filled with richly decorated arts and crafts objects in the form of rugs, cabinets, furniture and paintings. These, however, were traditionally kept in white rooms with dark beams and doors. The Norwegian painted interior on the other hand, could often be a piece of art in itself. The architecture, interior, furniture and decor were at all times perceived as one entity, and the interplay and integration between the different elements were carefully considered.

In earlier times, like elsewhere in Europe, decorated interiors were only to be found in churches and other grand buildings. The tradition of painting ordinary domestic interiors started around the beginning of the eighteenth century. This was a period of considerable development and economic growth in Norway. The era brought modernization and change to rural life, and was particularly open to artistic expression in all areas. With a burgeoning economy to support it, richly decorated artifacts and interiors became a way for people to express their newfound wealth.

The extent to which the interiors were adorned obviously varied, but it became commonplace to have an element of color in each room, and variations from room to room. Typically, there would be a blue room, a yellow room, a red room and so forth. It was only in the poorest households that almost everything remained unpainted.

Central to the new trend towards painted interiors, was the simultaneous development of the decorative style known as *Rosemaling*. The *Rosemaling* style incorporated Renaissance, Rococo, Baroque and Empire elements imported from the continent. These influences were adapted rather than copied outright. They were combined with local decorative traditions and personal style in the process. The Rococo styles that developed in Norway were thus in many respects more dynamic and expressive than the more formulaic style found on the continent.

Rosemaling was a highly adaptable decorative motif, it could be used on craft objects such as bowls and boxes as well as furniture, from chairs to cupboards and cabinets. This decor came to be used on interior details, or to cover entire ceilings, the insides of box beds or the walls of the home itself. It could be used on its own, as an abstract decorative pattern or in combination with figurative elements such as stylized portraits of people, mythical figures or a depiction of places.

Colorful rooms in a traditional Norwegian house: painting by Sigmund Aarseth, acrylic on canvas.

A 'framskåp' with traditional Rosemaling decor.

The *Rosemaling* tradition started in rural Norway, rather than in the cities, and was explored to its fullest in individual homes. Each district developed its own characteristic style, and there were enormous regional as well as individual variations. Some of the most prolific practitioners of *Rosemaling* were to be found in the remote highland valleys of Norway.

Towards the end of the nineteenth century, as the industrial revolution swept across Europe, *Rosemaling* lost its momentum as a dominant force in Norwegian decorative arts. By the early twentieth century it was considered an extinct art form. In recent years there has been a renewed interest in *Rosemaling*, but there is little education or training available in Norway. It is currently predominantly practiced on a hobby basis.

All the colors of the rainbow

There is no doubt that the natural environment and climate contribute to variations in interior design and decor. Around the mediterranean for example, cool white interiors and exteriors are surely the perfect contrast to the hot mediterranean climate.

In Norway on the other hand, one quickly comes to realize that the circumstances are quite different. In many parts of the country nature's own colors and decoration, in the form of plants, flowers, lakes and fields, are covered by a white blanket of snow six months of the year. The Norwegian tradition of richly decorated and vividly colored interiors is perhaps founded in a desire to bring some of nature's own sumptuous colors indoors.

The modern Scandinavian interior

The increasing dominance of modernism in Scandinavian architecture and design of the twentieth century must be seen in relation to the prevailing global trends as well as the economic and cultural situation during this time. Norway re-established

This colorful interior includes several decorative elements inspired by nature. The cabinet features a Rosemaling design with clear flower inspirations, and stylized clouds on the ceiling.

itself as an independent country in 1905, after being dependent on its neighbors Sweden and Denmark for the previous four hundred years. This transition took its toll on the nation's economy. Occupation during World War II and the subsequent rebuilding further strained the nation's resources.

In both design and manufacturing the emphasis shifted from individuality to uniformity, with a focus on mass production at a low cost. Simple and functional styles and the use of modern, high-tech materials such as concrete, aluminium and glass became economic as much as stylistic decisions.

In current times, decorative elements were reduced and stripped down to the basics and 'Scandinavian design' soon established itself as a trademark for functional but stylish products around the world. This deliberate break with the old stylistic elements has had a significant impact on Norwegian arts and crafts traditions. Many of the artistic skills that had taken hundreds of years to develop and refine were lost in the span of one generation.

This interior represents a mixture of seemingly conflicting influences, but with an interesting and individualistic end result. The fireplace, grandfather clock and cupboard are traditional ingredients in a Norwegian interior. The color combinations on the other hand are contemporary and fresh, so the overall ambience is quite urban and modern.

The continuation of a tradition

The latter part of the twentieth century was a period of renewed economic growth in Norway, this time fuelled by newly discovered oil resources and high-tech industry. In this environment the clean, uncluttered and undecorated style of modernism is often seen to be better adapted to modern lifestyles and tastes.

Having said that, Norway is a country where individuality and personal choice have always been important factors. Many people want more than just functionality in their homes. They wish to retain a sense of Norwegian traditions and national characteristics. The work featured in this book is the living proof of a renewed demand for colorful and decorated interiors.

This richly decorated farmhouse living room is a good example of a modern 'traditional' interior. A traditional color scheme has been used, and all of the woodwork has been painted, including the floor.

There have been requests for a book on Sigmund Aarseth's interiors for some time, and now that it finally has come to fruition, it is in some part due to Vesterheim, the Norwegian-American Museum in Decorah, Iowa. In 2003, they approached Sigmund to do a presentation on his painted interiors at their Symposium in April 2004. He soon realized that although he had painted a great number of interiors over the years, he actually had very little visual material to document this work.

In the fall of 2003, I travelled around both Norway and the U.S., retracing Sigmund's footsteps and visiting all the places he had worked. Along the way, I built up a substantial photographic record of about 1000 images to document the interiors he had decorated. A couple of months later, we were able to view most of his interior work in one place for the first time. Some of these interiors Sigmund himself had not seen since he first decorated them, in some cases decades earlier. Looking at them again with fresh eyes, he made many revealing observations. During our conversations, Sigmund explained the background and intentions of many of these projects. It is the essence of these conversations that we have presented here in this book — in Sigmund's own words, illustrated by my photos.

Gudmund Aarseth,
Edinburgh, Scotland June 2004

This painting by Sigmund shows a view across the Hjørundfjord, his birthplace on the West Coast of Norway.

Traditional decorative arts meet contemporary living

"I grew up in a rural fishing and farming village on the West Coast of Norway where I was born in 1936. Later I moved to Oslo, where I studied painting techniques for five years to become a Master Painter.

Simultaneously I spent all my spare time and resources taking part in painting and drawing classes. After graduating I worked for a while as an apprentice for a decorative painting firm in Oslo. I also met my wife Ingebjørg in Oslo and we relocated to the inland valley of Valdres in 1960. We have lived in this area ever since.

Over the years I has been involved in a range of artistic activities, although it is no doubt as a landscape painter that I am best known in Norway. I prefer to paint directly from life, so throughout spring, summer and fall I spend the majority of my time outdoors, capturing the ever-changing light and seasons of Norway on canvas.

During the long Norwegian winters the harsh climate prevents me from working outdoors, so during this time I have gradually developed a parallel career in the decorative arts. It is during these winter months that most of the interiors in this book were created. I have always had an interest in the folk arts of Norway, and in the early years my interior work was dominated by the traditional *Rosemaling* style. Since then I have developed a range of decorative styles derived from *Rosemaling* and other traditional decorative painting techniques."

"If I was to describe my work, I would say that it is clearly informed by the decorative painting traditions of my native Norway. I have a strong interest in retaining the skills and knowledge associated with Norwegian traditional arts, crafts and architecture. Studying historical pieces of Norwegian folk arts you often find an attention to detail and an aesthetic intuition, even in the most practical household objects, that is very rarely seen these days. It is this combination of practical skills and creative expression that I find particularly inspiring.

This does not mean that my own work always looks particularly traditional. I don't think copying what has been done before is the best way to keep such skills alive. Like the original *Rosemaling* artists of Norway, I work very impulsively, and rarely have a clear idea of exactly how the end result will look when I start painting.

Since my aim is seldom to replicate a historical interior, I am never too concerned about conforming explicitly to a particular historical style. It is more important to create a pleasing living environment that is suitable for the needs of its users. Modern lifestyles are not a hindrance for using traditional painting techniques. On the contrary, they can be an inspiration to come up with innovative solutions, often adapting well-known techniques and utilizing them in new and exciting ways. I believe that this approach can succeed in capturing the harmonious feel of a traditional Scandinavian interior more successfully than a direct copy could ever achieve.

My main concern when developing ideas for an interior is to define and create the ambience that I feel the space requires. This process might initially involve quite general notions such as 'light and open', 'formal and elegant' or 'casual and light-hearted'. My focus is on creating a continuity where the architecture of the room, the furniture, the colors, moldings and decor all combine into one harmonious unity. I try to develop a theme for the room or building, often based on its location and surroundings, or its current or historical use. As a project develops, the 'style' often evolves naturally with its foundation in these previous considerations.

Much of my work is domestic interiors where I collaborate closely with the owners throughout the process. Over the years I have also done a number of jobs in large commercial interiors such as restaurants, hotels and offices. In these circumstances I am often faced with a whole new set of challenges. In addition to the task of creating a pleasing, balanced and appropriately styled interior, there is likely to be a degree of compromise. The requirements for modern air conditioning and lighting systems, for example, must be taken into consideration, as well as health and safety issues and cleaning and maintenance requirements. Most venues can only afford to be closed for refurbishment for a very short time, making any job a race against time. Sometimes carpenters, electricians, painters and decorators all have to work side by side in order to meet the required completion date.

This book gives a flavor of the interior work I have done over a period of almost forty years. The majority of the interiors featured here are located in Norway, although I have also been lucky enough to get a variety of commissions in Sweden, France and the United States. I hope you will experience as much joy on your journey through this book as I have experienced while painting these interiors."

AT HOME

My own home in the Valdres valley is an old restored log house; the ground floor is more than 350 years old.

We moved this house to its current location in 1967. At the time we were renting a house, but there were only two months left before we had to move out. We already had this lot on hand, but not a lot of time if we wanted to build a house.

We soon realized that the only way we could get ourselves a new house this quickly, would be to find an old log house that we could move. Conveniently, log houses can be taken down and re-erected rather more easily than ordinary houses. This would at least give us a roof over the head in the short term, until we could afford something else.

This house stood on a nearby farm — it had been vacant for awhile and the owners were unsure what to do with it. With winter just around the corner and no time to waste, I bought the house for a symbolic sum.

Official bureaucracy was not as widespread in those days, so we were granted permission to start the building work immediately. Two months later the roof was on and shortly after we could move in.

Not everybody were convinced that it was such a great idea to spend time moving this old, virtually derelict house. Many doubted whether it would be possible to live in it at all over any length of time. Thirty years on, and a few extensions later, I think it is safe to say that they have been proven wrong!

The house may be antique, but we have made no attempts to treat it as a museum: it is an old house adapted to modern times. We have extended the house both towards the back and the sides, in step with our requirements and the growth of the family.

Over the course of thirty years, every room has been painted. The only exception is one bedroom (below) where the original hand-planed wood paneling has survived from when the house was new. There are a variety of styles — this is more a natural development over time than a conscious decision. To some extent I guess the house documents my own artistic development: this is where I often tried out new ideas, so some rooms inevitably reveal my professional interests at the time I decorated them.

▶ Decorated cupboard doors in the kitchen
▲ Large stencils dominate the 'weaving room'
◀ A door that combines folk art and modern influences
▶ A traditional hanging shelf in the kitchen
▼ The guest bedroom with built in beds and untreated wooden walls and ceiling.

The Hallway

In the hallway our visitors get a festive welcome with a painted floral festoon 'hung' along the ceiling. This style of decor is commonly known as 'Valdres roses' and is characteristic of the Valdres region where we live. The decor is not made with stencils, it is all painted freehand. Viewed up close you will notice that each bunch of roses is slightly different.

Closer inspection of the door which leads from the hallway into the living room (above left) reveals that it is unusually thick. It is actually two doors made into one and it is solid wood throughout. This door dates back to when the house was fairly new, more than three hundred years ago. The family who lived here at that time was known for their fierce tempers. One story tells about a family argument that resulted in the son being thrown out of the house. Undeterred, he tried to make his way back in with the aid of an axe he found in the shed! It is said that his father had this heavy-duty door fitted as a practical precaution after this incident.

The Kitchen

For a long time we had the kitchen (right) divided into two rooms. After adding an extension to the house some years ago, we decided to make it into one big room again.

Like most old log houses, the windows are smaller than what you would usually get in a modern house. The kitchen only has these two windows, so there is not very much daylight coming into the room. This prompted our decision to give it a lighter, 'sunnier' appearance by painting it yellow. The decorations on the doors and cupboards are also done in a light style and color.

Yellow is, in fact, not a particularly common kitchen color in Norway, at least not in this region. On the farms in the area it was very common to paint the kitchens light blue. Many believed that this color helped to keep the flies away.

The kitchen ceiling had previously been covered by smooth boards. The old planks underneath saw the light of day again during our refurbishment. It was immediately apparent why we had originally chosen

to cover them up. The planks were rather rough and uneven, with noticeable cracks between them. It would have taken days to fill all the cracks, so we almost considered covering it all up again.

In the end I decided to decorate the ceiling exactly as it was. The decoration can thus be said to serve a dual purpose here. The bold brush strokes effectively disguise the uneven surface and make the cracks significantly less prominent.

Notice the characteristic shelf suspended from the beams above the kitchen table. Such shelves are common features in traditional kitchens and dining rooms in the Valdres region. They are very useful for storing bowls, jugs and much, much more.

The Weaving room

We have started calling the room above 'the weaving room' after it became the home of this old loom. The room is one of the newest additions to the house, created when the bathroom and hallway below it were extended. There is a touch of continental sophistication to this room — the color scheme is reminiscent of a Rococo or Baroque interior. The stenciled friezes are also highly original features, although I took the inspiration for the patterns from traditional folk art designs.

As with all the other additions we have made to the house, I personally made the architectural drawings for the extension above. Even at this stage I tried to keep in mind how we might paint the room once it was finished. This allowed me to get the details of the interior perfect for later decoration.

Bedroom

The bedroom (below) was originally a separate little log cabin. We moved it onto our lot and connected it to the main house a few years after this was erected.

We have kept the high gabled ceiling in this room. To further emphasize the open feel, we painted the ceiling bright blue with stylized white clouds.

Expanding on the idea of "waking up under a blue sky", I painted the walls green with a stylized pattern of foliage and red berries along the ceiling. The paintings on the walls are also mine, they are from a series of folk art inspired pieces that I created prior to painting this room.

Library/office

Before we added this new extension to the house, I had seen several examples of 'earth sheltered homes' in the United States. The point of this concept is to retract the house into a mound or hillside in order to conserve heat and save energy. This idea seemed to lend itself to the valleys of Norway, where the winters can often be extremely cold. We took advantage of the naturally sloping hill towards the back of our property and partially receded this extension into the ground. (It is the structure to the left on the photo on page 16).

We have not kept the newer additions to the house as traditional as the original parts. In this room the brick walls are painted white, continental style. The doors and windows follow the conventions of brick architecture; they have been inset in the walls without wood frames.

The ceiling ornament features a number of different elements. The fishing boat represents my childhood in a fisherman's family on the West Coast. There's also a painter's palette, which I assume requires no further explanation. To the right is a 'family tree' with five figures below it to represent our family. The cryptic symbols in the center are the little known 'Mørske runic alphabet', which is only known from the West Coast region where I grew up.

Over a period of several decades, I have decorated virtually all the doors in the house. The styles range from traditional *Rosemaling* to figurative art and modern abstract ornaments. Among the many human figures on the doors around the house you can sometimes recognize members of our family.

A warm welcome

First impressions are always important, and in architectural terms it is surely doors that provide the first impression of a building or a room.

Every place requires something different, so here is a small selection of some of the many different solutions I have come up with over the years.

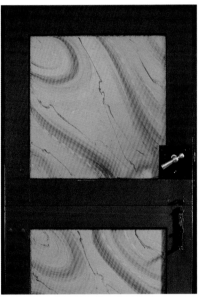

The traditional farmhouse

Idstad farm is just around the corner from where we live. It is one of the most traditional farms in the area. During the summer it hosts visits by tourist groups from both Norway and abroad.

There are two large houses here, which is not unusual for a farm like this. In earlier times several generations commonly lived side by side under the same roof. As times got more prosperous a second building was often put up next to the main house. The parents usually moved to this house when they passed the farm on to their children. The fairly anonymous exterior is typical of farm houses in rural Norway. Unexpected surprises may await you in such places: this building, for example, houses one of the finest collections of antique cupboards in the valley.

We used a reddish pink color in the living room as well as on the kitchen doors and wainscoting (right). This color is typical of farmhouse interiors, so much so that it is commonly known as 'old pink' in Norway. When the kitchen was refurbished we discovered a substantial empty

▼ The text panel on the wall at the end of the dining table states the names of the family members, a short grace in Old Norwegian and the year the room was decorated (1982).

space above the original ceiling, so I suggested creating this coffered ceiling (right). The added height gives a modestly sized room a considerably more spacious feel.

Marbling

The light patterns seen on the doors, door frames and ceiling are known as 'marbling'. This is one of the most common decorative techniques in Scandinavian interiors, but also widespread throughout Europe. As the name suggests, marbling was originally used to imitate marble. In many grand buildings on the continent, great effort has been put into making it look as naturalistic as possible. In Norway marbling quickly developed into an expressive decorative technique in its own right, rather than 'imitation painting'. This kitchen is a typical example: the similarity to veined marble is apparent, but without attempting a naturalistic imitation. The execution of the marbling technique can be varied greatly. In Norwegian marbling the sweeping lines often have as much resemblance with flowing water as with veined marble. Sometimes even the stylized landscapes in Edvard Munch's paintings spring to mind. Different styles of marbling can be seen many places in this book, among others, see pages 18, 52 and 80.

A common characteristic for two story buildings like this one is a large upstairs reception or sitting room, reserved for formal occasions. This was typically the grandest and most elaborately decorated room in the house. This upstairs room (right) I have decorated in a style typical of the Valdres region. For the unusual, gently rounded ceiling I have used a restrained, symmetrical style of Valdres *Rosemaling*. The walls feature the floral garlands known as 'Valdres roser' along the ceiling, stylized 'chinoiserie' landscapes and boldly marbled wainscoting.

Tradition lives on in a modern house

Traditions are a part of everyday life in this household. Magny is head of the Norwegian board of folk costume research and Rolf was director at the Valdres museum of local history when they purchased the house.

The house, on the other hand, was a thoroughly modern prefabricated house. This was contrary to the type of house they initially had in mind, but they wished to reintroduce some of the sense of local history and traditions that they felt were missing. The first step towards achieving this was to carry out certain structural modifications. Most radically, the entire roof, which was originally fairly flat, was raised. This created a more spacious attic room with a window facing the valley, as can be seen in the exterior photo to the right.

Inside, the blue marbled door frames and red furniture contribute to what I would describe as a typical Valdres interior. The living room had rather dull,

▲ A tranquil mid-winter view across the fields towards the house and the old barn.

smooth fiberboard walls rather than the wood paneling you would find in a traditional house. We applied a light blue/green glaze coat to these walls, which leaves traces from the brushstrokes as can be seen above. I find that this lively texture resembles the look of natural wood.

The painted flower garlands are a type of decor that was sometimes used in this way in the larger farmhouses in the region. The flowers are more naturalistic than in most Norwegian folk art and this style is perceived to be characteristic of the Valdres valley. It was based on Baroque influences from continental Europe, so very similar styles of decorative painting can be found in other European countries. Particularly in Austria and Northern Italy I have seen many examples of what I know as 'Valdres painting'.

The cupboard on the previous page is decorated in an early style of *Rosemaling*, which is symmetrical and fairly monochromatic. I did it in this style to match an old cupboard in the same room, which is painted in a similar style.

▲ These 'tiner' (bentwood boxes) were commonly used to store flatbread, cakes etc. Here they are conveniently stored on top of a cupboard.

Molor Farm: Modern living in an old house

The main house at this small farm had fallen into disrepair when the current owners bought it. Many people would no doubt have been tempted to demolish the house and build an entirely new one. Instead, Eli and Eivind gave the house a much needed face lift. It has been extensively modernized, but this is done in such a way that new and old merge seamlessly.

I participated in the restoration process by doing the architectural drawings for the refurbishment and extension. The color schemes and decor for the interiors were developed in close collaboration with the owners.

He is a freelance documentary film director and photographer, and recently built a film studio across the road from the main house (right). The location commands an enviable view of Lake Volbufjorden. I designed this building, which put me in a privileged position — I could design every detail of the interior with later painting and decorating in mind.

In this modern building the decor is more modern in style than in the main house. The tradition of painting all woodwork has been maintained. Notice the figures that appear on either side of the doors to the right. When viewed from the hallway the woman faces you while the man is turned away. From the inside it is the other way around. The year of construction, 1999, is incorporated into the decor on the entrance doors in the background.

▲ For the ceiling in the old dining room I have used a muted color scheme to complement the walls and furniture in untreated wood.

◄ The photograph on the wall above the bench is a nice touch; it is not an old family photo as it might appear, but a photo of King Haakon V and Queen Maud of Norway from the early 1900s. It was very common at the time to hang such a picture in your home.

Dragon style

This old farm is superbly located on a secluded hillside in Valdres. The main house is now the home and office of an interior designer. This fact contributed to making it a particularly interesting project for me. The most challenging room in the house was the sitting room (far left) with a complete set of 'Dragon style' furniture. The Dragon style developed during the 19th century in a climate of national pride as Norway struggled for independence from Sweden — a goal finally achieved in 1905. Its development coincided with several major archeological finds from the Viking era, which sparked renewed interest in this period of the nation's past. Revivalist in nature, the Dragon style is largely based on the ornamental styles of Viking arts and crafts, and has gone in and out of favor over the years.

We complemented the geometric shapes of the fabrics and the square seats of the chairs by dividing the ceiling into square panels with a pattern of geometric stencils based on heraldic and medieval inspirations.

At the other end of the house, the aristocratic dining room (left) provides an interesting contrast to the Dragon style room. The elegant combination of oak furniture and burgundy walls is here crowned by a ceiling decoration around the chandelier. It is painted entirely freehand with a drybrush technique on the lightly textured ceiling surface — this looks a lot easier than it is!

A bachelor's home fit for a king

This sitting room with stunning gilt Rococo furniture would not look out of place in a French manor. It is actually to be found in a restored Norwegian farmhouse. The set of highly characteristic antique furniture became an obvious starting point for creating a light and refined Rococo interior.

On the ceiling we used stencils both for the patterned border and the large ornament in the center. Stencils are of course most commonly used when a pattern needs to be repeated a number of times, like for the border here. On this occasion I chose a stencil for the large ceiling ornament too, in contrast to the ceiling on the previous page. This was predominantly done to retain a firm and classical look, reflecting the elegant lines of the furniture.

Note that the walls appear to be covered in yellow silk wallpaper. A close inspection reveals that this is actually paint; stripes of gloss varnish applied over a yellow base-

coat give this luxurious appearance. This might seem like an elaborate and expensive solution, so let me put it into perspective: both the walls and the ceilings in these rooms had been covered in inexpensive masonite, and the total cost of all paintwork is much less than what re-paneling with good quality wood paneling would have cost.

The furniture in the adjacent dining room (above) is equally impressive, with a full set of *gyldenlær* (gilt embossed leather) chairs. Chair coverings of this type were particularly popular in Scandinavia at the beginning of the 18th century, and although these chairs are more recent, finding a complete set of them like here is very rare.

The inspiration for the decor in this room came partially from the elegant chairs, which demanded a grand solution, and partially from the chinoiserie decor on the door of the antique cupboard which dominates the room.

The Chinoiserie fashion (*Kineseri* in Norwegian)

To Europeans in the 17th and 18th century, China was a distant and exotic land that fascinated and intrigued people. Europeans, at the time, were in fact fascinated by all things exotic and often made little distinction between China, Japan, India or even the West Indies. They often simply referred to all of these as 'the Far East'. In the 18th century trade increased between Europe and the Far East. Large quantities of textiles, wallpaper, porcelain, furniture and craft objects were imported to Europe. Much of it was made especially for the European market. The demand for such products was in fact so great that it also prompted a substantial output of European reproductions. This 'Westernized Orientalia'—European artifacts inspired by or imitating Far Eastern arts and crafts—are commonly known as *Chinoiserie*. The term is also often used specifically in reference to the stylized landscapes which are a key decorative element in traditional Chinese arts and crafts. The chinoiserie fashion coincided with the emergence of Rococo in France, and was an important element of that style.

The chinoiserie fashion also had an influence on Norwegian arts. This is a typical example of how styles from the continent were adapted and integrated into local folk art traditions. By the time the trend reached Norway it was obviously far removed from its Far Eastern origins. The landscapes created in Norway were not always particularly 'exotic'. They were, however, usually imaginary landscapes, and drew on whatever inspirations the artist had. They would often feature trees, animals and buildings not native to Norway. Such landscapes were typically used on the panels of doors or cupboards. Sometimes they were also done on a grander scale, on the walls themselves. (See facing page.)

It is interesting to note that Norwegian decorative artists usually executed these landscapes monochromatically, typically in muted blues like it is done here. This is reminiscent of traditional Chinese watercolors and woodcuts, although the Norwegian artists most likely didn't know about these at the time.

▲ This detail shows how large parts of the wall paintings have been created using a natural sponge. A few simple outlines and highlights have been added with a brush at the end. The clouds on the ceiling (right) complete this stylized landscape.

▼ A detail from another 'chinoiserie' interior. This is from the room featured on page 25.

Expressive traditionalism

The fresh and spontaneous decor in this farmhouse has its roots firmly planted in Norwegian traditions. It is one of the early interiors that I decorated, at a time when I was still predominantly working within existing folk art traditions.

There are few active practitioners in the field of traditional decorative arts in Norway today, much of what is being produced are reproductions or adaptations of original work and these often have a polished and impersonal look which fails to retain the personality of the original. Kari, the housewife in this household, is a colorful and expressive person who made it clear that she was not fond of slick 'imitation' *Rosemaling*.

My response to this request was to adopt an original and highly expressive technique that I had not tried before, in the execution of the decor. This can be seen most clearly in the ceiling on the second floor (top right). After quickly sketching the main forms using a piece of chalk, I filled in these scrolls using a large brush filled with diluted paint. Rather than letting the brush strokes follow the movement of the scrolls like conventional *Rosemaling* technique would prescribe, I used the brush

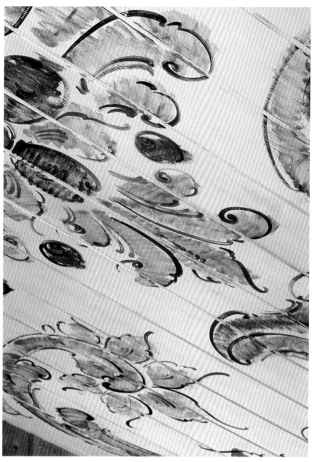

transversely, roughly defining the shapes. Finally, darker outlines were added. The result is lively and full of character. For examples of ceilings decorated utilizing a more conventional technique, see pages 49 and 97.

Ola, Kari's husband, wanted to keep the walls unpainted, whereas Kari and I would have been happy to paint them. By retaining some transparency in the ceiling decor I have ensured that it does not appear too dense and heavy in combination with untreated wood paneled walls.

As I started painting the doors, Kari decided that Ola had deserved a painting of a nice girl on one of the doors. I first painted this door (left), but when Kari saw it she said: "oh, yes, that is a very nice girl, but I think she is perhaps a bit too nice and obedient for my husband!" On the next door I painted another girl, this time with a more Latin temperament. This door can be seen in the photo on the previous page. I did it very quickly, which contributes to the dynamic look. The couple says that they both like this particular door more and more as the years go by.

A rural retreat with an international flavor

The barn burnt down many years ago on this old farm which overlooks Lake Slidrefjorden in Røn, Valdres. The main house has survived and is now the rural retreat of Danish minister and author, and my good friend, Erik Rostbøll and his wife Kirsten. They are world travelers in the true sense of the world and have been just about everywhere that you can think of. This house in the Valdres valley has become their main residence, although they usually escape the Norwegian winters by going south, for example to Malta. The building to the right in the photo above is a private chapel that the couple has had erected, the main house is on the left.

The couple's international outlook and wide-ranging interests are evident all around the house: there are artifacts from all over the world, merged in an individualistic and eclectic mix. Erik's brief to me when I first came here to paint the dining room was simple: "Do it any way you like, just don't do it so that when my old aunt comes up from Denmark, she'll say it is cute!"

The dining room is open towards the kitchen and has a large, wood-fired iron stove in the fireplace. A wrought iron chandelier above the table and decorative swords on the wall contribute to a rustic, almost medieval ambience. Both the walls and the furniture have been given an antique stain over the basecoat. This mutes the colors somewhat and leaves traces of the brush that give a handcrafted and genuine appearance.

On the wall there is a tapestry reproduction of a famous medieval fresco in the Palazzo Pubblico in Sienna, Italy (left). Dating back to 1330, this is one of the first medieval paintings that shows a landscape with realistic perspective. I found my inspiration in the patterned horse trappings and decorated the ceiling with bold brush strokes. The heraldry inspired patterns are executed in deep, muted colors. Around the edges there is a darker border made up of religious symbols, which were developed in collaboration with the owners.

The Drawingroom

It is no coincidence that there is a distinctly British feel to this sumptuous drawing room. The couple lived near Cambridge, England, for many years, and here the deep leather armchairs, antique oak furniture and carpeted floor have brought the atmosphere of an aristocratic British residence to their Norwegian home. The tall dark chair behind the writing desk was originally made for John Milton, the 17th century British epic poet. The couple's connections to Malta are also represented through the Maltese crosses appearing in the stained glass windows.

Both the furniture and the stained glass windows with carved surrounds are reminiscent of the 'Elizabethan' and Neo-Gothic styles once so popular in Britain. To perfect the ambience of the room the ceiling was completed with Elizabethan style decor. Apart from being true to this style, the colors we chose reflect the colors found elsewhere in the room. The ceiling matches perfectly the burgundy, brown and gold book spines that are prominent both in this room and in the small adjacent library. The circular moldings in the corners of the ceiling were turned and carved by a local craftsman.

This is an example of an interior where I worked closely with the owners to create the ambience they were looking for. They had a lot of ideas of their own, and one of my challenges was to find visual forms to express these ideas.

On many occasions when I am asked to decorate an interior, it is because people have seen what I have done somewhere else. Some people feel that they know my work well enough to give me complete freedom to do whatever I find appropriate. This can naturally be just as challenging, and require a lot more planning than if they already have specific ideas and wishes. Most people naturally want some involvement in creating the right feel of the rooms they will be living in every day.

Heidi Fossheim has been my skilled, hardworking and light-hearted helper on many projects at home and abroad. It is no surprise, therefore, that the interiors in her own home are highly accomplished and individual.

For the livingroom above, I assisted in choosing colors and planned and drew the stencils used for the ceiling. Heidi did all the stencil cutting and the actual paintwork herself. At the end, I came back to do the simple thistle inspired designs that adorn the cupboard doors and the paneling on the back of the horse-shoe shaped sitting area. Notice that absolutely all of the woodwork, including the floors and the furniture, has been painted. I feel that this interior is particularly harmonious.

▲ The living room features a highly original seating solution. Just like the cupboards on the far wall, this built-in sitting group next to the fireplace is entirely self-made and fully integrated into the interior.

It is no coincidence that the bedroom above looks more Mexican than Norwegian. Heidi had seen something I did on a Mexican theme in the United States years earlier. She liked the lush colors and bold patterns so much that she wanted her bedroom in this style. She painted the room in her preferred 'Mexican' colors, and I did the decorative frieze and ceiling ornament for her.

It was also Heidi's idea to create a decorative frieze on the floor in the room below. As in the livingroom on the facing page, Heidi did all the paintwork herself, making this an easy and unusual job for me. Since I designed the stencils but did none of the practical work, I only saw the fruits of my labor long after the room was finished.

▼ It might seem a shame to spend so much time decorating a floor, which after all, will get a fair amount of wear and tear over the years. Having said that, this room is not used as much as the rest of the house. Moreover, the decorative frieze is kept close to the wall, where there will be a lot less wear than in the center of the room. In addition, it has been given a coat of hard-wearing varnish.

Rural Norway meets continental Italy

These images are from a fairly recently built house in Vestre Slidre, Valdres. In new houses that are not traditional in their layout and construction, I don't always find it natural to use entirely traditional color schemes and decorative styles.

A traditional Norwegian interior often employs a wide range of colors in each room. There is usually one dominant color — typically red — but you might find combinations of reds, blues, greens and yellows all in the same room. The cottage overleaf or the bedroom on page 53 are good examples of this use of color.

In this home on the other hand, I have used a much more restrained color scheme. This is an attempt to give the rooms a more classical, timeless ambience. Each room, therefore, features colors predominantly from one part of the color spectrum. This can be seen both in the living room and in the kitchen above.

Tall, wood-fired stoves are prominent features in several of the rooms in this house. One can be seen in the living room above, and a similar one stands in the hallway, on the other side of this doorway.

The owner actually has a collection of these antique, elaborately ornamented stoves. I adapted some of the ornaments and used them several places in the interior. The cupboard doors in the kitchen all feature stenciled ornaments adapted from the cast iron panels on one of the stoves. In older times, interior artists often looked to such stoves for inspiration.

When this house was being built and fitted out, the owner chose marble floor tiles imported from Italy for the hallway (next page, bottom photo). I have used various 'marbling' painting techniques in many of the interiors featured in this book, but I am pretty sure that this is the only place where there's real marble too!

When a room has a unique characteristic or feature, such as the flooring in this hallway, I always try to take it into account and work with it. This is absolutely one of the most important factors in creating a harmonious interior. It does not matter how accomplished or beautiful each element is in its own right; the elements must complement each other and not compete, or it will never work.

The overall color scheme in the hallway was very much informed by the color of the marble tiles, with a light, muted pink as the base color. I also used a dark, almost black blue around the panels on the doors. This complements the iron stoves as well as the dark squares of the marble flooring.

On the hallway doors, I created Baroque inspired designs with peacocks and lush flower bouquets. This kind of colorful, symmetrical decor is probably more widespread in the alpine regions of Europe than in Norway. In a sense, this room therefore becomes a melting pot for Norwegian and Italian influences.

The designs I have created here may not be typical Norwegian, but they are certainly still rooted in traditions. It is not unusual to find exotic birds, animals and other foreign influences in Norwegian folk arts. It is easy to imagine that people at the time did not always want to see just what surrounded them in everyday life.

The only things that were never depicted in older times, were supernatural creatures such as trolls and gnomes. Trolls are now of course very popular motifs in Norway, but I always try to avoid painting them and come up with alternative solutions. I find that this motif has been overused and destroyed through its frequent use in commercial mass-produced souvenirs.

It is easy to forget that when the interiors we now perceive as 'traditional' were created, they were often anything but. They were certainly not based on set templates and I think their variety and innovation were much greater than most people realize.

A home away from home...

Many Norwegians without doubt consider owning a *hytte* (cottage) by the sea or in the mountains a necessity rather than a luxury. Offering a welcomed escape from everyday life, some will retreat to their cottage most weekends. Some cottages being built these days are virtual palaces with all the amenities of the modern world, but the idea of retreating to a different place, detached from the modern world, still has its obvious appeal. Many therefore prefer their cottages to be as traditional as possible, providing a contrast to their main house, that might be very modern in style.

This cottage is located at the end of a dirt road, overlooking a lake deep in the Hallingdal mountains. Some cottages only have the bare essentials for living, but this one is of the more luxurious variety. With five bedrooms it can comfortably accommodate family, friends and relatives.

Despite the amenities of modern living, you can still often find yourself at the mercy of the elements in such locations. We were working in this cottage in the middle of winter while a blizzard passed the area. It left us practically snowbound for the whole week we were there. Luckily a group of British Royal Marine soldiers were on winter training nearby at the time. Thanks to them we got the car dug out of the snowdrifts and the engine running again!

There are some interesting architectural solutions in this building. The full height of the gabled ceiling has been retained above the dining room area. An open 'gallery' overlooks it from the loft upstairs (previous page). The huge area of the ceiling represented a significant challenge. There were no beams or rafters to provide firm borders. I was concerned that any decoration I did would appear too busy without sufficient framing. We solved this by adding narrow moldings to create three separate panels in the ceiling. They complement the paneling around the gallery/balcony and tie the room together.

The kitchen (far right) features a variety of decorative elements. The words on some of the cupboard doors serve both a practical and a decorative function: they are recipes for some common local dishes.

▲ The storage cupboards in the hallway have been transformed into a picture wall based on local legends and stories.

► Interiors in the Hallingdal region were traditionally extremely elaborately decorated. Often virtually every inch of every surface was painted and adorned with Rosemaling, marbling or other decor. This tradition is reflected in the decor we did in this cottage.

▼ A view across the nearby lake at night.

i frå Hallingdal, med sal og med hest og med

There is a certain air of rural Norway over this house, despite its location in a suburban residential area. It merges with the landscape on the outskirts of Norway's second city Bergen. Low turf roofs and modestly sized windows gives it the impression of being a modest country cottage.

Interestingly, this house is an exact replica of a house I decorated a few years earlier. It was built by a friend of the owners, and they liked it so much that they wanted their own! The only modification required to adapt the house to this lot, was to reproduce the architectural drawings back to front. Since I had painted and decorated the original house, they invited me to come and decorate their home too. Overall it is very similar to its original 'twin house', although I rarely do exactly the same thing twice. Here I was given a rare second try, and perhaps I am more satisfied with the result I achieved this time around.

▼ The hallway functions very much like a stylistic link between the exterior and the interior of this house. the deep red and bottle green are typical Norwegian interior colors, whereas the symmetrical, classically influenced door decorations hint at the style of the reception hall (top right).

When you enter the large reception hall you realize that the house is in fact quite a lot bigger than its outward appearance has led you to believe. This hall is an impressive space in its own right, with a number of paintings and prints displayed on the walls. We would run the risk of compromising the lovely, spacious feel if too much decor was applied in this room. The light and elegant color scheme emphasizes the feeling of space. A very subtle and classical stenciled frieze underlines the elegant and aristocratic feel.

There is no natural light coming into the hallway that leads to the bedroom wing (right). It was quite a narrow and dark space, at least in comparison to the lavish reception hall. Yellow walls have helped to give it a lighter, 'sunny' appearance, while the green wainscoting links it to the reception hall. This corridor, with its many doors, ended up being perhaps the most original and impressively

▲ The reception hall gives easy access to all parts of the house; to the left is a small TV room and to the right is the kitchen. Straight ahead is the bedroom wing towards the back of the house, and at the front of the house there is a large sitting room.

decorated part of the house. The doors here feature a number of different decorative techniques; stylized floral hangings on top, 'chinoiserie' landscapes in the center and marbling in the bottom panels. The overall aim was to give a light, open impression to make the corridor seem less enclosed. The marbling at the bottom is therefore a lot lighter and dynamic than what proper 'imitation marbling' would have been. The sweeping lines reflect the landscapes above. A consistent, fairly monochrome color scheme has been used in order to retain a unified look.

The majority of this decor was done without a brush—I used a crunched up cloth and 'wiped' the paint onto the doors. This is an extremely efficient way of creating the kind of 'drybrush' effect you see here; I could paint ten of these doors in one day. In the small hall between the master bedroom and the rest of the house (below), we used different colors and decor.

▼ the master bedroom (right) has a uniformed guard — painted on the door.

▼ The decor on the hallway doors is continued on the doors of the built-in cabinets in the bedroom.

This guest bedroom, with its richly decorated box bed and built in cabinet, is kept in the best traditions of Norwegian folk art. The room will often be used as a kids' bedroom, so the owners wanted to evoke something of a fairytale atmosphere.

The panels on the bed and wardrobe feature something of a hybrid between *Rosemaling* and marbling. *Rosemaling* typically consists of strong scroll shapes with a lot of movement while marbling uses simpler, less expressive forms. I had planned to do the panels in a traditional marbling technique, but since this had already been used extensively in the hallway, I ended up creating the more expressive variation you can see here.

The inside of the bed is also decorated; a mounted knight at the foot-end of the bed completes the fairytale theme.

A room with a view

The view from this living room takes in the whole valley below. From its hillside location it overlooks the town of Fagernes. No one can see into the room from outside, so there is no need for curtains. The panels between the windows have instead been embellished with a light thistle-inspired floral motif.

This room has a large expanse of ceiling, and my main objective was to find an imaginative way to integrate it with the rest of the room. As anyone can imagine, decorating directly onto a ceiling like this is extremely demanding, not least physically. On this occasion I was able to paint onto cutout boards instead. These were subsequently mounted onto the ceiling, and stenciling was added around the panels. Using such panels has the added benefit of breaking up the flatness of the ceiling, dividing it into

smaller areas. Apart from the light leather sofas, the furniture here is mainly unpainted wood. These colors were picked up on and repeated in the ceiling decor to produce a tasteful and refined unity.

We decided to combine the warm and earthy colors of the floor and ceiling with cool walls. This has in my opinion resulted in a calm, entirely modern room. I feel that without my background in traditional decorative arts it would have been much more difficult to accomplish this.

An artist's home

The home of my painter friend Gro is an old house, in fact it is registered as a protected building by the conservation authorities, due to its historical significance. The house has a lot of personality—much has been allowed to remain unchanged over the years. It doubles as a private gallery, so most of the walls are densely hung with paintings. Because of this the interiors didn't require much additional decoration.

The most important element in this kitchen is the dark, low wainscoting. This color continues around the door frame and moldings, which adds weight to the lower parts of the interior and helps balance a busy interior. The spring green walls are topped by a lightly painted grapevine that is subdued enough not to compete with the paintings.

AT WORK

'Valdres Gardsbryggeri', Valdres Farm Brewery, was established in 1999. It is most probably the smallest commercial brewery in Norway.

Located at 2300ft above sea level, it can also no doubt lay claim to being the highest altitude brewery in the country. Unlike the United States, Norway is still dominated by a few very large breweries, with just a small number of more local breweries around the country. This makes *Valdres Gardsbryggeri* quite unique, and so far it has been very successful in carving out a niche for itself in this very competitive field.

The brewery came into being after three friends ran out of beer during a party (according to their own account at least). They agreed that the safest way to prevent this from happening in the future, would be to start their own brewery! They set about realizing this plan with a great deal of enthusiasm, but probably unaware at the beginning of just how much work it would take to achieve this goal.

▲ This tranquil winter scene shows the brewery building set against the backdrop of snow-covered pine trees. At one time the production building (right) housed the sheep at this small highland farm.

First of all there was obviously all the practical work of creating fully capable production facilities. Some equipment could be acquired secondhand, while other parts, like the actual brewing vat, had to be custom made. On top of this, there are complex regulations on production of food or drink in Norway, and even stricter regulations regarding the production and sale of alcoholic beverages. After three years of planning and preparation, the brewery was finally at the stage where they could start test production.

The production capacity is modest, at about 15,000 gallons per year, and the brewery sometimes struggles to meet demand. In addition to distribution locally, and increasingly further afield too, the brewery bar opens to the public every Friday night.

This interior is a good example of just how much the ambience of a room is determined by the color and decor. Warm, subdued earth tones and solid handmade wood furniture give the space a rustic atmosphere. The boldly executed decor has quite a traditional feel, mainly due to the colors used. I have used *Rosemaling* as a frame for a multitude of human figures.

A wall painting in the hallway (below) shows an 'oppskok'. This kind of social gathering was a common thing when I was growing up. It often took place when all the men in the neighborhood had been helping out on a big job. This could be digging the foundations for a new house, tiling a roof or gathering the animals.

To make up for the extra work you could then brew some beer and gather people around for a tasting when it was ready. This always took place in the brewing cellar; the fresh beer was poured directly from the brewing vat. There was very much a pub atmosphere, people would sing or play instruments or tell stories.

In close-knit communities this had a valuable social function too; it improved neighborhood relations and prevented potential feuds.

Production methods

At *Valdres Gardsbryggeri* production is very much a manual process, based on old methods which have been adapted for commercial use and modern equipment. The brewery remains the only one in the country to use this brewing method on a commercial basis.

The brewing takes place in the room that also acts as a pub and function room — the brewing vat and fermentation tank are located directly behind the bar. (above left). This adds a great deal of character and authenticity to the pub.

In contrast to the widespread lager and pilsener beers, the brewery produces so-called top-fermented ales. These are characterized by a full and robust flavor. There are two types of beer currently in production. One is a golden, crisp ale, the other is a darker ale with a particularly rich flavor, achieved by using five different types of malt.

This small chapel, located near the ski resort of Beitostølen, is known as *'Lyskapellet'*—the Lightchapel. It has been erected in the grounds of a health and recreation resort for disabled people, in memory of the center's founder Erling Stordal.

▲ With a maximum capacity of around forty, the 'Lightchapel' is popular for christenings and small weddings. My daughter Halldis was married here in 2002. During the summer the chapel is also used for conventional church services.

The building is traditional in its log construction, but unique in its pentagonal shape. The interior is dominated by a large stained-glass window (previous page) designed by the late Norwegian artist Ferdinand Finne. It was his last major work of art. The window was manufactured in Germany, while the floor is made of natural slate slabs sourced locally.

A soothing and refined feeling is evoked by a 'heavenly', cobalt-blue ceiling with sparkling golden stars. Thick beams form a huge pentagonal star suspended above your head, only touching the corners of the room. The beams are entirely covered by goldleaf, which brings a lush, glowing ambience to the chapel. At the same time this allows the logs to retain much of their natural character. The cracks that have formed have not been filled in, and even the texture of the wood can be seen through the gold.

I enlisted the help of my brother Kjell Arne on this job. He has extensive experience of restoration work in old churches and is something of an expert in applying gold leaf.

A light and expressive vine pattern is painted on top of the gold. This is a motif sometimes used in old Norwegian churches. The vine decor is done in Viridian Green and Alizarin Crimson. These are naturally very transparent pigments, which gives the hues an intense, radiant glow when painted on top of gold leaf like this.

Bergo Hotel is one of a number of hotels in the ski resort of Beitostølen. Some of the warmth and comfort of a domestic interior has been introduced into these basement rooms. It was previously a night-club, now the room features a large dining table, a built-in bed and a fireplace. It was mainly intended to provide additional space for families with children to play cards, read books or simply relax. The decor is fairly folkloristic, with *Rosemaling* on the ceiling and figures from a local legend adorning the walls.

This hallway (right) leads from the reception down to the sitting rooms. People in traditional costumes populate a rural landscape on the walls. In this enclosed space with no windows, even stylized landscapes such as these create a certain illusion of space. The more refined and colorful figures in the foreground add a feeling of depth, which gives the hallway a significantly less contrived ambience.

In the main room, comprehensive decoration combined with careful lighting has entirely transformed the ambience. These interiors use some of the most basic paneling available, as can be seen in some of these photos. This has little impact on the end result — you might even argue that it contributes to the rustic, authentic feel.

The box-bed (left) was intended to be filled with pillows and fairytale books to make it a tempting den for children, but the hotel has not gotten around to completing this space.

The panels on the wall depict the local legend about a knight who fell in love with a girl from a rival family. He went to the neighboring valley where she lived and persuaded her to run away with him. They did not get far before the escape was discovered, and they were pursued on horseback by supporters of her father. The knight's horse was carrying both of them, so their followers were steadily closing in. The last panel shows how they made a narrow escape by jumping over a gorge so wide that nobody dared to follow. The story is generally true, and the gorge is now a local tourist attraction.

Quality Hotel Fagernes is superbly located by the shores of Lake Strandefjorden. This large conference hotel in the town of Fagernes incorporates a cafe and a restaurant as well as a number of conference halls and meeting rooms.

Built in the 1960s, the hotel originally had a very modernistic exterior, complete with flat roofs, untreated concrete and pebble-dash façades. At the time, this architecture matched the adjacent town hall. The town hall retains this appearance — it is just visible at the left-hand edge in the photo above. The hotel got its new look after a comprehensive face-lift in the late 1990s. The addition of balconies and gabled terracotta-tiled roofs dramatically transformed the hotel's appearance.

In the dining hall (right), dark hues and brass details set the tone in this stylish serving area, which would not look out of place in a French chateau. The ceiling in here is the single greatest improvement that we made. I got the carpenters to create these slanted panels where we could put large stencils.

► The refined look is re-inforced through the use of Fleur-de-lis ornaments in gold on the cupboard doors. This emblem was historically associated with the French royalty.

'Klukkarstogo'

The hotel had tried several times to create the right ambience for the cafe above, but never quite felt that they had achieved their goal. When they got me involved they had decided they wanted to make it more representative of the region. The director did not care much for *Rosemaling*, so we decided to settle for a much simpler, rustic style.

Carpenters created these built-in stalls on the premises according to my drawings. The rose patterns on the sides of the stalls are common in local wood carving. On this occasion there was no time and money to get them carved, so I painted them instead.

One day, while working here, I forgot my work shoes at home, so I borrowed some old shoes at the hotel. They had rather slick soles, so I naturally slipped of the stepladder and bruised my right shoulder. I had to paint the remainder of the ceiling with my left hand. In a sense I guess this made it easier to retain that rustic style with little dynamic in the strokes!

'Grillstuene'

Compared to the dining hall on the previous page, the hotel restaurant below has a more intimate, domestic ambience. This interior was again created in close collaboration with the carpenters.

The low ceilings in this space emphasize the 'homely' atmosphere. In fact, they were a practical requirement in order to disguise some unsightly air-conditioning shafts which ran along the ceiling. At either end of the room we created more open spaces with coffered ceilings, as can be seen below.

The aptly named Blue Hall is adjacent to the dining hall on the previous spread. A variety of freehand painting, linework and stenciled ornaments have been combined to create a richly decorated but elegant interior. The restrained color scheme ensures that the hall retains a light and noble feel that really stands out.

At the time when I decorated this room, the hotel kept a huge display of artificial flowers on the table in the middle of the room. This inspired me to create the painted floral panels around the walls. The original flower display is now of course long gone, but the flowers I painted still remain.

In my opinion this is the most accomplished and original room in the hotel. However, you can never please everybody — a speaker on the first meeting to be held here after the refurbishment, scolded the hotel for "ruining" the room in this way!

A refreshing place to study and read

This is the local public library in the district where I live. It is not very often that I have been asked to do large and modern public buildings, so this was an unusual and challenging job.

The building has been designed with a light and open 'courtyard' in the middle of the room. This space has a slightly raised ceiling and darker, slate-colored flooring. Like most libraries, the rest of the library has a somewhat cluttered feel, so this is an interesting architectural solution.

Book shelves cover virtually all wall spaces apart from the top three feet of the walls. This made it natural to create a frieze that goes all the way around the room in this area. The stencils I created for this frieze are among the most complex I have made. They consist of up to eight colors that each must be cut as a separate stencil. These are then applied one after another. On a practical note, when I do stencils around a room like I did here, I usually make several similar looking stencils with slightly different widths.

With a bit of planning you can then always get combinations that fit the width of the wall perfectly.

Nowadays we use transparent plastic stencils and apply the paint mainly with small paint rollers rather than brushes. This simplifies the process a great deal. I was lucky enough to escape from the time-consuming task of applying the stencils. My oldest daughter Halldis is an interior designer, and she took over the practical work of actually painting them.

One of the few decorative symbols traditionally associated with libraries that I know of, is the palmette. We used this stylized leaf pattern on the columns surrounding the courtyard area (second photo from the top). I have previously seen it used on the exterior of classically styled libraries. I imagine that it goes back a long time, maybe all the way back to antiquity and the first libraries. Perhaps it symbolizes the growth of knowledge when used in this context?

On the few wall spaces that are not covered by book shelves, we have created various little features. In the space next to the magazine rack I have reproduced a poem by a local author, and next to the checkout desk there is a 'literature tree'.

The tree has its roots in the old Norse saga literature, represented by the large book at the bottom (left). The runic writing underneath is a reproduction of an inscription discovered in an old church not far from this library. Each leaf on the tree contains a short quotation. Towards the bottom there are quotes from classic Norwegian writers such as Ibsen and Hamsun. Further up the quotes are from more contemporary Norwegian literature and from world literature. I got my youngest daughter Marit, who has studied Norwegian literature, to select these quotes and write them on the leaves.

In public buildings such as this one, there is an obvious emphasis on functionality, which makes it quite different from working in a private home. There are many more people involved, so you cannot always make quick decisions there and then, like I prefer to do. This can slow the whole process down and does not always suit my very impulsive way of working.

This little church is our local church, a short walk from where we live. In many ways it is an archetypal Norwegian church, built of wood and painted white.

The small, dark log construction which can be seen to the left of the church is called a 'stupul'. This building is basically a free-standing bell tower. Such buildings were commonplace in older times — the bells were housed here rather than in the church tower itself. This *stupul* is a lot older than the church, it houses medieval bells that are only used at funerals.

As long as I can remember, the entrance hall to our church has remained rather dull and gray. A few years ago we had a minister who was quite a creative guy. He enjoyed painting in his spare time and thought it was a real pity that this nice little church had such a drab and impersonal hallway.

The story of just how we came to decorate it starts shortly after he arrived in the parish. He soon approached me to ask if I would decorate the entrance hall. I reminded him that the church is protected (by the national architectural conservation authorities). I expected having to go through a lengthy process to get permission to carry out any modifications.

Our minister, however, had the feeling that the people in charge at the time had little interest in such details. He was certain that if he tried to raise the matter through the official channels, it could go on for

years without anything ever coming of it.

He decided that his own common sense was more to go by than the formalities, so he asked again if I would decorate the entrance hall if he painted it first. He knew, of course, that after all there was nothing in the entrance hall that qualified for conservation, so no real damage could be done.

We painted the room in a subtle color scheme with light rococo clouds on the ceiling and biblical symbols in gold on all the doors. Everyone in the parish was happy with the result. The church authorities still knew nothing about it, so they did not worry or complain about it either.

It was only much later that the district provost came on a visit to the church. He was rather surprised to find the entrance hall transformed, since he had not heard anything about it. Clearly uncertain how to react, he started listing the authorities that should have known about this but didn't; "...so the conservation authorities have not been consulted, I have not been consulted... oh, never mind — after all it is beautiful!"

'*Filefjellstuene*' is a guest house and restaurant high up on a mountain pass along the main road between the inland of Norway and the West Coast.

The place is halfway between the cities of Oslo and Bergen and close to both the Jotunheimen national park and the Sognefjord. This makes it an excellent base for excursions and outdoor pursuits both in summer and winter. Accommodations are provided in a number of separate little cabins, while the main building has a dining hall (above) for the guests that doubles as a restaurant.

The rural, not to say remote location, high up in the Norwegian mountains means there is an abundance of quality raw ingredients available. This includes fresh seafood brought up from the West Coast and local meats and specialties from the mountainous inland. The venue has quickly developed a reputation for the quality and originality of its food — it was recently awarded a prize as one of the best places to dine in Norway.

It was my daughter, Halldis, who first got the commission to design the interior for this dining hall, when it was built a

▲▼ The walls with windows and white panels above and below are actually mobile partition walls. They are extremely well integrated into the interior, and enable a layout with the dining hall in the middle and a meeting room and TV room for the guests on either side.

couple of years back. Although it is a large space, I think it succeeds very well in retaining a warm and intimate atmosphere with plenty of personality.

I was asked to do the wall decorations on either side of the entrance. They are done in a style that I find has a lot in common with traditional pictorial tapestries, particularly in the way they combine purely patterned areas with figurative elements. The figures have a flatness and simplicity of form which also resembles pictorial weaving techniques.

The fairly rigid style used here prevents the decorations from becoming too busy and dominant, even if they are done on a large scale. A color scheme that is carefully matched to the rest of the interior also helps. The main aim on this occasion was after all to integrate the decor into the interior rather than creating free-standing pieces of art that would be the focal point in the room.

An unspectacular partition wall has become an interesting feature in this dining hall. It is located in the block for catering and hospitality courses at *'Valdres Vidaregåande Skule'*, Valdres Highschool.

This room is used to train students who will go on to work in the hotel and restaurant business. The school therefore wanted to create something of a restaurant ambience. This would give both students and staff a more inspiring and realistic work environment. The school management was also considering making the room available for public functions in the future.

Like in so many schools, the rooms were pretty drab and the budget was limited. Part of the plan for the refurbishment of this hall was to replace all the furniture. It was all nice wood furniture, but it looked very worn after many years of heavy use.

I had the idea that we should first simply try to bring all the chairs to an auto body shop and have them spraypainted. This turned out to be no problem and it gave the chairs an entirely new lease of life. It saved the school a lot of money and at the same time lessened the strain on the decorating budget.

◄ I created pairs of two identical panels on this partition wall. The stylized wheat patterns are most complex in the center and gradually simpler towards the sides. This helps create a focal point in the design.

▼ My designs on the wall are inspired by the ornaments found on the chinaware used in this hall. This type of china with its characteristic blue patterns is very common in Norway.

The entire end wall in the hall (bottom) is a 'concertina style' partition wall which can be opened up to make the hall even bigger. These kind of mobile or removable walls are usually not very pleasing to the eye. Luckily, this one could at least be painted without any problems.

One option would be to simply make it look like an ordinary wall. I tried instead to make a feature out of it. Rather than disguising the fact that it is made up of hinged partitions, I created a panel on each partition and filled these with slim, elegant ornaments.

It would have been too monotonous to use the same design idea throughout a large hall like this, so on the wall above the tables I came up with another style of ornament. These designs were created quite impulsively, and I think of them as "stylized *Rosemaling*". You could see them as a cross-breed between the wheat patterns on the partition wall and traditional *Rosemaling*.

A taste of rural Norway in the center of Oslo

These interiors are the basement rooms of a modern student hall at the University of Oslo. I was contacted after it was decided to turn them into gathering rooms to be used for festive occasions. Prior to this the rooms had all had entirely different uses.

The housing manager had family ties to the Valdres region, so she had the idea of transforming these into "The Valdres rooms". Our brief was therefore to create an atmosphere of rural Norway in the center of Oslo — on a very limited budget.

The first room you enter (above) has the feel of a countryhouse living room. It has untreated wooden floors, a traditional open fireplace and domestic cupboards on the walls.

It was the large hall adjacent to this room (right & overleaf) that represented the greatest challenge. It is very long and narrow, and only has low windows on one wall. Up until then it had therefore often been used as a storage space.

We eventually decided to turn this room into a richly decorated 'Knight's Hall'. There is in fact historical evidence of a knight living in the Valdres region in medieval times. This is how the idea of a 'Knight's Hall' first occurred to me. It also meant that we didn't actually deviate very much from the 'rural Norway' theme.

Before we started painting, inexpensive panels were added in the originally flat ceiling to create a gentle curve.

In Norway we often call such curved ceilings 'chest ceilings' because they resemble the gently curved lids of traditional Norwegian chests. In this room it matches the shape of the windows too (previous pages). A cabinet-maker created a table out of thick planks that fills the length of the room, and made matching wooden benches along the walls.

The hall is not an imitation of a medieval interior, but merges heraldic and medieval inspirations with folk art references to create a rustic, authentic ambience. It was transformed from a basic storage space into an exclusive banqueting hall almost solely through the use of paint.

Like much of my work, these designs are based on the idea of complementary, or contrasting, colors and shapes. This is particularly evident in the 'Knight's Hall'. The 'royal blue' wainscoting with its very

simple linework is topped by a lively acanthus frieze on a golden background. The loose red scrolls on the ceiling are surrounded by firm, blue frames.

The wall space above the acanthus frieze has been divided into pictorial panels that take some inspiration from medieval woven tapestries. The figures are depicted in quite a 'flat' style, and the spaces between the figures have been filled with patterns and heraldic symbols. Note the gilt crowns adorning the 'posts' between the pictorial panels. Matched with the Renaissance-style painted draperies along the walls, they contribute to an exclusive, almost ceremonial feel.

Between the first room and the 'Knight's Hall' there is another small space (right). We made this small hall serve as a transition space between the domestic feel of the first

room and the grandeur of the main hall. It is open towards the first room and has a smaller, arched portal towards the main hall.

The checkered floor in this area is not marble slabs or tiles. We painted the pattern onto the floorboards in order to separate the rooms on either side. The walls have stylish Fleur-de-lis ornaments reversed out of a striped pattern. All these elements contribute to make the space serve as an antechamber to the larger hall.

In the last room (above) there was no existing furniture, nor was there much money left in the budget for furniture. We quickly decided to make it into a 'ballroom' — then it wouldn't need much furniture after all! We decorated the room in a light and refined Rococo color scheme with subdued pink and purple hues. The two chairs and the chandelier were bought cheaply at a secondhand furniture shop.

◄ These decorations serve much the same purpose as stained-glass windows in a chapel. After all there are no windows in the walls of this building, only skylights. The slim decorations give the space a significantly less enclosed feel.

A place for meditation and contemplation

This small building, which has been dubbed 'the meditation house', is part of the large Vesterland hotel complex near Sogndal. The house contains a sauna, a Jacuzzi and this 'meditation area'. It features a wood-fired stove, a small water feature and a music system. I was brought in to provide an element to stimulate the visual sense. These decorations are predominantly intended to complement and emphasize the meditative mood, so they are entirely abstract with calm blues as the dominant colors.

Bringing nature inside

This converted barn is situated at the entrance to the Utladalen valley. This is a dramatic, narrow valley popular for trekking and climbing. The house acts as an information portal to the area and the valley behind. Around the room there are exhibition panels with information on the history and geology of the area. This end wall is a visual journey through the valley, from the agricultural plains at the bottom up to the highest snow-covered mountain peaks.

I find that this piece has certain similarities with a style of monumental decorative painting that developed in Norway in the postwar years.

My son Gudmund, who has designed this book and did the photography for it, came along on this job. He did the painting to the right that covers the space where the barn doors used to be. It shows how hay used to be carried in through these doors while the building was still being used as a barn.

Decorative art for the modern world

The original Norwegian *Rosemaling* that adorned interiors more than 200 years ago, was created specifically for the houses of that age. Construction methods and architectural styles have obviously changed a lot since then. There are not very many contemporary buildings being built where I find that traditional *Rosemaling* is entirely appropriate.

In the interiors where *Rosemaling* was first used, a number of elements contributed to the overall ambience. Door and window frames, wainscoting, beams and skirting boards were all painted and incorporated into the decorative design. The large number of firm, balancing elements in these interiors allowed the first Rosemalers to use an abundance of dynamic scrolls in their designs. In many modern interiors, these elements are either much less prominent or removed altogether.

I have for some time been aware of the requirement for a decorative style that is true to our time — something that is

▲ This is the simple and modern staff canteen in the offices of a distribution company. It is many years since I painted this abstract decoration on the end wall, but I still think it is well suited for this interior.

▲ This swimming pool is located in the same health resort as the chapel on page 62. Within a simple and low-key interior, this wall is a firework of color.

better adapted to the materials, furniture and characteristics of a modern building. In response to this, I have put considerable effort into trying to revitalize and modernize the traditional decorative arts. On these pages you will find examples of some of the contemporary decorative styles that I have developed over the years.

The room on the previous page is a good example of such a contemporary, pared down interior. When I did this decoration, I included a number of straight, vertical lines in the design. This makes up for the lack of a firm visual framework in the interior itself and balances the dynamic shapes in the design.

The mural in the swimming pool above is a more recent piece. Here, the format itself stresses the horizontal within an interior with many vertical and horizontal lines. I have therefore used more dynamic, round shapes in this design. When the pool is not in use, the mural is reflected in the calm surface of the water. This doubles the impact — since the piece is entirely abstract, it looks just as good upside down!

Rosemaling is similar to the works of many classical fine artists in that it relies heavily on the principles of complementary, or contrasting, colors and shapes. Round shapes can be counterbalanced by combining them with straight or square shapes. Similarly, all colors have a complementary, contrasting color on the opposite side of the color wheel. Blue is a complement to orange, red to green, yellow to violet and so on.

In the 1970s, I started doing progressive experimentation based on the way these principles were used in traditional *Rosemaling*. I specifically analyzed how the dynamic relationships between different shapes had been utilized. Based on these observations I started stripping my compositions down to their basic core components. I tried to simplify and exaggerate them by creating studies that consisted of simple round shapes contrasted by completely straight lines. This resulted in a surprisingly modern look. The blue canvas reproduced

▲ These decorations are at Valdres Highschool. In fact it is the corridor just outside the hall featured on page 78.
The decoration is done in the spontaneous and little planned style that you often find in folk arts. The colors on the other hand, were carefully planned beforehand. I aimed for a lighthearted and youthful expression in this piece.

▲ This is one of the more stylized studies I have done. It contains the 'C' and 'S' shapes typical of traditional Rosemaling, but the overall feel is a lot more modern. There is also the addition of straight vertical lines.
▼ This piece is not actually all that different in its core composition, but the much more expressive brushwork gives it an entirely different feel.

here is one of my studies from this period.

At this time I had started holding *Rosemaling* classes in the United States, and these studies were very effective in explaining key compositional principles to my students. I have since used these very formal studies as the basis for less rigid styles with more expressive brush-work. Usually I just put on some music and start painting what comes to me at that moment. One brush stroke leads to another, but I always keep complementary shapes in mind. All the pieces that I have created on canvas have really only been intended as studies for decorations that could be reproduced on a much larger scale in a modern interior. Some of these designs I think would work well on their own on a large wall, much like the pieces on the previous pages.

In Norway, I find that we are still 'recovering' from modernism—many modern buildings are still very minimal in their use of color and decoration. The official arts organizations are very strong, and they usually control the art commissions for all new public buildings. In addition, they generally have quite specific ideas about what kind of art they want to endorse. This makes it difficult for an 'outsider' like me, who is not a member of the established organizations, to be considered for such commissions.

The majority of my decorative work is commissions in homes and private businesses. In these cases I often get a free hand and can complete the job quickly and at a reasonable price. In public buildings you often feel encumbered by committees who sometimes have very little aesthetic knowledge. At times so many plans, sketches and planning meetings are required that I lose my inspiration before I have even started painting. In my experience all this time spent in the planning stage makes the end result substantially more expensive, but not necessarily any better. In fact I find that I often have to make so many modifications and compromises that it creates a poorer result from my point of view.

I think I can consider myself lucky that I don't often get involved in such big jobs. Although they could be lucrative, I'm not sure if it would be worth it.

BRINGING NORWAY
TO AMERICA

Ett lite stykke Norge — 'A little piece of Norway', is the advertising slogan used by one of the most popular Norwegian chocolate brands. The same expression could easily be used about this complex, which brings a distinctly Norwegian flavor to the woods of Wisconsin.

This secluded vacation home in Door County has over the years evolved into a treasure-trove of Norwegian arts and crafts. This is the first place that I tried my hand at interior painting in the U.S., back in the 60's. I was asked to come and decorate some ceiling beams, so I drove across from Minneapolis in a borrowed car. It was after dark when I got to Door County, but there was a light visible through the woods. When I saw a large Norwegian flag in the window, I knew I had come to the right place.

The two small log houses to the left are Norwegian 'stabburs', or storage buildings. They were actually built in the Telemark region of Norway, brought over to the U.S. in pieces and re-erected here. Since these are real Norwegian houses, I felt that I should respect their origins and try to stay true to the traditions and decorative styles characteristic of the Telemark region.

Houses in Telemark were typically very richly decorated — it was not uncommon to do elaborate painting and decoration even in the *stabburs*. In both of these houses, we painted the log walls as well as the ceilings. The top floor of the larger *stabbur* (above right), makes an excellent spare bedroom. I decorated the large ceiling here in a Renaissance style, like you can find it done

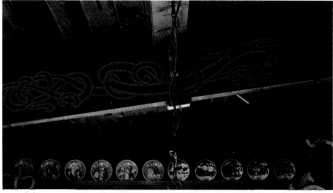

in some old Norwegian churches.

In the main house (above and right), Dean, the owner, had initially only planned to have the beams of the gabled ceiling painted. I knew that it would be both tricky and elaborate to decorate the sides of beams this high up, so I asked if I could paint the ceiling between the beams instead. This was quicker and easier than painting the beams, and has much more impact since it is more visible from below. The large red painting on the wall (above), is also one of my pieces, although it is a more recent addition. Some call these paintings *"Sigmalings"* — they represent one of the decorative styles I have developed with a foundation in traditional *Rosemaling*.

The dining room (above right) used to be a porch that has since been built in and integrated into the house. The dark and rustic style gives this room a medieval feel that in fact reminds me a bit of a Norwegian stave-church. The 'dragon style' ornament I created on the dark beam above the table is inspired by the viking-style woodcarvings that commonly adorn stave-churches.

► This cozy reading corner is flanked by painted wood carvings and a panel featuring a poem by Norwegian poet Arne Garborg.

▼ The stave-church at Borgund has a characteristic dark exterior and dragon-style ornaments as well as crosses on the roof.

Scandinavian dining in a Scandinavian environment

The Ann Sather restaurants of Chicago are a well-established chain of Swedish restaurants in the northern area of the city. The restaurant above, popular for its lingonberry pancakes and cinnamon rolls, is located next to the Swedish Institute in Andersonville. This is an area of Chicago traditionally inhabited by Swedish immigrants. Scandinavian culture is still represented through a number of Swedish restaurants and delicatessens in addition to the Swedish Institute.

It was something of a coincidence that first put me into contact with the Ann Sather restaurants. A friend of mine, Mary Parker, had been approached with the request of decorating the interior of this restaurant. She felt that she did not have the experience to do this alone, so she got me involved.

Debbie, the manager of the restaurant, had already decided that she wanted something based on the theme of 'Nils Holgerssons underbara resa genom Sverige' — The Wonderful Adventures of Nils Holgersson. This is a much-loved Swedish children's story written

▲ Nils Holgersson enjoys his ride on the back of a goose high above Skåne in southern Sweden.

▲ Nils arrives in Visby on the island of Gotland.

by Selma Lagerlöf in 1906. It tells the story about the mischievous country boy Nils, who travels the length of Sweden on the back of a goose after being dwarfed by an angry gnome. The panels in this restaurant illustrate the highlights of his journey.

One of the problems associated with decorative work in restaurants is that they only want to stay closed for the shortest possible time. Speed and efficiency is therefore absolutely essential. The grand re-opening had already been planned when I arrived to decorate this restaurant. I immediately saw that there would be too much to manage in the time allocated without extra help. I turned to Sallie Haugen DeReus, who came to my rescue. We have since collaborated on all the Ann Sather venues featured in this book.

People often think that it is the main features, like the panels here, that are the most elaborate part of a job. Actually the surrounding details and trimmings, like the frieze along the ceiling and the linework around the panels, are usually more time-consuming. This work has to be done very accurately or it will inevitably end up looking like a rush job.

Ann Sather Restaurant, Belmont

This is the original and largest of the Ann Sather restaurants. It has several rooms on the spacious first floor, as well as a number of variously sized rooms on the floor above. The current look of the restaurant is the result of three different periods of work. While working here I have had good help from Sallie Haugen DeReus, Mary Parker and Knut Øystein Bakken, among others.

The main room is dominated by large quantities of dark oak paneling. (It was actually an undertaker's office once upon a time, although there's little left to remind you of that these days.) The paneling was originally combined with very light colors, which made the oak look dark and cold.

I chose a warm red as the main color with *Rosemaling* decor in burgundy red and gold. This lends a warm glow to the oak paneling too, and makes the overall ambience a lot warmer and more welcoming.

The restaurant remained open throughout the decoration work, so many of the regulars followed the progress with great interest. Many were impressed by the new look of the restaurant, including mayor Richard M. Daley, who came for the opening. As always though, it is impossible to please everybody. One regular customer greeted the new decor with the exclamation "Well, now it looks just like an old ugly tie I used to have!"

The problems you encounter when decorating such large rooms are likely to be practical as well as artistic. Here I had to crawl on top of cabinets and balance on top of stepladders to get access to all the areas I needed to decorate. At the same time I had to try and keep a natural and rhythmic flow in the brushstrokes.

Since this is the 'original' Ann Sather restaurant, owner Tom Tunney was rather keen to maintain a Scandinavian theme.

For the second room we developed a 'royal Swedish' theme in collaboration with a design consultant. The main elements of the decor at that time were portraits of Swedish kings and their coat of arms on the walls.

I had my reservations about this very formal approach. It didn't seem to suit the room all that well and I found that it made the furniture look much too ordinary. On the other hand, it can be very difficult to judge just how well a theme will work before the whole room is actually completed. It is only when you start getting feedback from the general public that you can really begin to assess just how successful a job has turned out to be.

The room was later judged to be too austere; it was not as popular with the public as the other rooms. When I came back the next time we changed it completely. The current decor, featured here, is very light and light-hearted in style. Inspired by a classical music piece called 'Invitation to a dance', this wall shows groups of people preparing for a festive occasion.

The rooms upstairs at Ann Sather, Belmont, are truly multi purpose spaces that are used for anything from meetings and conferences to parties and even work-out sessions. It was necessary to decorate these rooms in styles that are neutral enough to fit any occasion.

When time is short, I try to utilize speedy techniques that nevertheless give a rich impression. In the first of these rooms, the 'Swedish Room' (right), I painted monochromatic Swedish castles, based on old etchings, in a drybrush technique directly onto the wall.

The large adjacent hall (above), suitably known as the 'Norwegian Room', is dominated by Norwegian landscape paintings. I painted these in Norway and brought them over to be mounted in the restaurant. The landscapes are interspersed with mirrored panels that I initially thought would look out of character with the present ambience of the hall. It actually turned out quite well; when you are seated here you can view the landscapes on the opposite wall reflected in the mirrors.

▼ This small room without windows was previously mainly used for storage. We discovered that it had this barrel ceiling disguised by a low board ceiling, and it was almost as an afterthought that we decorated the room. It is now the most popular room in the restaurant for small meetings and gatherings.

Ann Sather Cafe, Southport

This small cafe opened a few years back in the relaxed residential area of Southport, northern Chicago. It was pointed out to me that one characteristic of the Southport area is that many local residents take an active interest in cultural events such as concerts, theatre and opera.

Incidentally one of the walls had a niche where the wainscoting almost gave the feel of a stage (above), so I thought we could try to create an opera theme out of it. (In the smaller Ann Sather venues it is not deemed so important to have a specifically Swedish or Scandinavian theme.)

There was much local interest when rumors spread that there was an Ann Sather opening. When people heard about our plans for the decor, some even came back to lend me books on opera and theatre to provide inspiration.

On the wall opposite (right) we created an audience for the operatic performance. At Ann Sather they like to include something to reflect their focus on offering freshly prepared food with quality ingredients. Consequently, I painted a village with a food market where fresh produce is being brought in behind the spectators.

▼ Chicago these days is a very multicultural city. I suddenly became aware that I have always only painted blond people in my decorations. To make up for this I painted a dark prima donna here and for the first time consciously made the audience multicultural.

Ann Sather, Broadway

This cafe has a youthful clientele, so it was important to keep the decor fresh and contemporary. Apart from this, we started out with no specific brief, so instead we went for a walk to soak up the atmosphere of the neighborhood.

The largest wall was a rough brick wall that I knew would be tricky to paint. I solved this by using small paint rollers rather than brushes, which was the only way to do long 'brush strokes' with some rhythm and flow on this surface. I created an impressionistic, Chicago-inspired cityscape (above left), which offers an interesting interaction between the decor and the surface of the brick wall.

After completing the decor, new high-backed seats have been installed along the walls. The backs cover the bottom third of the wall completely, so it is a much 'amputated' version of my decoration you can see here today.

On the other surfaces I used a contrasting 'hard-edge' style and technique, inspired by a Matisse exhibition we saw at the Art Institute of Chicago the day before. We created simple, asymmetrical shapes executed in fresh, provocative color combinations (above right).

Vesterheim Norwegian-American Museum

The Norwegian-American Museum in Decorah, Iowa is the largest ethnic museum in the United States. It has a large collection of artifacts accumulated over more than a century of collecting. All aspects regarding the emigration and settling of Norwegians in America have been documented here.

I have had links with the museum for many years. As part of the museum's program of workshops I have been teaching *Rosemaling* classes on and off over a period of almost forty years.

When Vesterheim trustee, Dean Madden, donated a new administration center to the museum, I was commissioned to decorate the interiors as part of the donation. I was given a free hand, and it proved to be among the most challenging jobs I have ever had.

The decoration work was focused on a large gathering room that was to be used for conferences, meetings and so on. In the corridor that leads to this room (above) I wanted to create the impression that the viewer is on an open porch, surrounded by Norwegian landscapes and people.

The people are dressed in different national costumes from all around Norway. Such costumes are typically worn at festive occasions, and sure enough, when you get to the end of the corridor, you find a couple about to get married. The clothing worn by this couple (above) is characteristic of my home region on the West Coast of Norway.

In the main room I had initially planned to use the emigration of Norwegians to the U.S. as a theme, but this seemed a little too somber. The house is separate from the actual museum building, so we thought we could allow ourselves to create something quite fresh and light-hearted.

After discarding the emigration theme I was uncertain what to do, but this was instantly resolved when I got a book for Christmas about the ancient Norwegian calendar system known as the '*primstav*'. The *primstav* was basically a flat wooden stick about two feet long that represented the duration of the year. Along the length of the stick it featured a mixture of Christian, pre-Christian and pictographic symbols to represent '*merkedagar*'. These 'marked days' were days of particular significance, either

relating to seasons, harvest, popular super-stition or religious festivals. From medieval times up until the late nineteenth century the *primstav* played an important part in ordinary people's lives.

The *primstav* captures in vivid detail the daily life of Norwegians around the time of the emigration. Many of the traditions were kept alive until the mid-twentieth century, and also brought along to the new home-land by Norwegian immigrants to the U.S.

In the gathering room the symbols of the *primstav* are reproduced alongside short rhymes and proverbs. These made it easier for people to remember the meaning of the individual symbols. Above this frieze we created one panel for each month where the full significance of the symbols below is illustrated. The month of April, dominated by the Last Supper, is shown above right.

The visual style of these decorations is inspired by early pictorial tapestries, and in particular by the 'Baldishol Tapestry', an early medieval tapestry discovered under the floorboards of the Baldishol church in Hedemark, Norway in 1879. The discovery of the *Baldishol Tapestry* prompted a renewed interest in early weaving techniques.

Vesterheim has several reproductions of this tapestry in its collection.

One of the problems when decorating a large room like this is to get the timing right. Rather than completing the panels one by one, I worked my way around the room again and again, building up more and more detail. This way I could finish at any point, and all the panels would still be done to the same standard and with the same level of detail. I worked alongside my long time collaborator Sallie Haugen DeReus when decorating this space — she did much of the time-consuming work such as the lettering and the symbols.

Along the bottom of the walls (overleaf) we simply added painted 'draperies' to achieve an overall balance in the room. Considering the elaborately decorated ceiling, it was important to add some 'weight' to the bottom of the room. Painted draperies like these are a feature often found in old reception halls and manors in Norway.

The last time I was at Vesterheim, I showed a group of fifth-graders around the room. It was interesting to see that the decorated room also appeals to the younger generations, as was my hope and intention.

Sammendrag på norsk

HEIME

Heime hjå oss *(side 16-21)*

Huset som vi bur i flytta eg hit i 1967. Sidan den gong har vi bygd på fleire gonger etter kvart som det har vore behov for det. Dei fleste romma er dekorerte i ulike stilartar. Dette er ikkje nødvendigvis eit bevisst valg, men snarare ei naturleg utvikling. Ofte har eg 'prøvd ut' nye idear her som eg seinare har vidareført i andre interiør.

Idstad gard *(side 24-25)*

Idstad er ein av dei mest tradisjonsrike gardane i nærleiken av oss. Stova er her fargesett i 'gamalrosa', medan kjøkkenet er blått slik det var vanleg på gardar i eldre tid. Under oppussing av kjøkkenet vart det oppdaga at det var mykje tomrom over himlinga, så vi utnytta dette til å skape eit 'kistetak'.

Vi har brukt mykje marmorering i desse interiøra, særleg på dører i kjøkkenet, men også på bjelkane i stova. I Noreg vart marmorering tradisjonelt brukt som ein mykje meir ekspressiv teknikk enn på kontinentet, der det ofte vart lagt mykje arbeid i å etterligna marmor.

Karlberg *(side 26-27)*

I dette ferdighuset har dei fleste romma både tak og veggar i huntonitt. I stova har vi skapt eit ganske tradisjonelt interiør med raude møblar og lyse blågrøne veggar. Vi laserte veggane for å få ei meir levende overflate, og eg måla 'Valdres roser' langsetter taket. Dette er ei type dekorasjonsmåling som tidlegare var mykje brukt i Valdres.

Molor Gard *(side 28-29)*

Molor Gard er ein gamal gard der hovedbygningen har vorte kraftig renovert og modernisert. Eg hadde eit godt samarbeid med eigarane her både når det gjaldt teikning av påbygget, uttaking av fargar og dekorering.

Åsen gard *(side 30-31)*

På denne garden har dei ei 'finstogo' med møblar i dragestil. For å skape eit interiør som passar til denne stilen, ruta vi opp taket på ein måte som tek att forma på stolseta. Takpanela har heraldisk-inspirerte ornament.

Stova i den andre enden av huset er meir klassisk i stil, her har vi måla burgunderraude veggar kombinert med ein frihandsdekorasjon i taket.

Øvre Hande gard *(side 32-35)*

Denne gardsbygningen i Røn, Valdres, har to flotte stover. I den første stova er det antikke rokokko-møblar, så her har vi skapt eit gjennomført rokokko interiør. Veggane, som ser ut som dei er dekka av gult silketapet, er faktisk berre gulmåla plate-veggar med striper i blank lakk på toppen.

Den andre stova har eit fullt sett av stolar i gyldenlær. Her har vi skapt eit interiør med kineseri-landskap på veggane. Kineseri trenden spreidde seg frå kontinentet til Noreg på 1700-talet. Som namnet tyder på, var det handverk importert frå Kina som var opphavet til denne typen dekor. Kinesisk kunsthandverk er ofte dekorert med landskapsmotiv som inspirerte europeiske handverkarar til å måle etterligningar. I Noreg fekk mange herskapshus og storgardar rom med kineseri-landskap på veggane.

Øvre Skjefte gard *(side 36-37)*

Dette er eit av dei tidlege interiøra eg måla, ein gong på syttitalet. Kari og Ola, som bur her, ville gjerne ha eit tradisjonelt interiør, men likar dårleg glatt 'imitasjons-rosemåling' som ein så ofte ser. Spesielt taket er derfor grovt måla med kraftige penselstrøk som går på tvers av hovedformene.

Rostbøll *(side 38-41)*

Dette gamle småbruket i Røn, Valdres er no bustad for prest og forfattar Erik Rostbøll, som har flytta hit frå Danmark. Huset ber preg av at det er verdsvande folk som bur her — gjenstandar frå mange reiser over heile verda er samla her. I spisestova er stilen rustikk, nesten middelalderaktig.

Kontoret ved sidan av har eit tydeleg britisk preg — paret budde i mange år i nærleiken av Cambridge. Taket er dekorert i 'Elisabethansk' stil, med fargar som står bra både til møblane og til dei mørke bokryggane med gullskrift.

Nerre Kvissel gard *(side 42-43)*

Heidi som bur her, har hjelpt meg med mange dekorasjonsoppdrag både i inn- og utland. Ho har gjort nesten alt det praktiske arbeidet her sjølv, eg har hjelpt til med uttaking av fargar, teiking av sjablongar og litt frihandsmåling. Det mest karakteristiske her er kanskje golvet i 'gamlestogo', som er dekorert med ein breid sjablongbord i raudt og gull.

Nordsveen gard *(side 44-45)*

I nye hus, slik som dette i Røn i Valdres, synest eg sjelden det er naturleg å prøve å lage eit heilt tradisjonelt interiør. Eg vil beskrive resultatet her som forholdsvis klassisk og tidlaust, med ei blanding av norske tradisjonar og kontinentale påverknader. Særleg entreen med barokk-inspirerte blomsterdekorasjonar og påfuglar på dørene, kunne like gjerne ha vore i Italia eller Østerrike.

Bergsjø, Hallingdal *(side 47-49)*

Denne hytta på fjellet i Hallingdal er dekorert i tradisjonell Halling-stil. Skråtaket i stova var for stort til å fylle det med ein dekorasjon, så vi delte opp denne flata med listverk og fekk tre dekorerte felt.

Åsane, Bergen *(side 50-53)*

Dette huset i Åsane kommune utanfor Bergen er faktisk identisk med eit hus på Fagernes, bygd av ein kjenning av eigaren. Han likte dette huset så godt at han ville bygge eit som var heilt identisk. Eg dekorerte huset på Fagernes, så eg fekk dermed oppdraget med å dekorere her også.

Huset er ein god del større enn det ser ut til utanfrå, med ein stor hall midt i huset. Denne hallen er enkel og klassisk i stil, medan soveromsfløya er rikare dekorert med meir tradisjonell fargesetjing. Eg gjer sjelden ting heilt likt to gonger, og resultatet her vart kanskje minst like bra som i det 'originale' huset.

Berg, Fagernes *(side 54)*

Frå denne stova er det flott utsikt over Strandefjorden. Ettersom det ikkje er innsyn utanfrå, er det ikkje bruk for gardiner. I staden har vi laga dekorative strå-motiv i felta mellom glasa. Det var særleg det store flate taket eigarane ville ha dekorert her. Eg måla dekorasjonar på plater som etterpå vart monterte opp i taket. Dette gjev også ein relieffverknad som hjelper til å bryte opp den store flata. Fargene i taket reflekterer tregolvet, dei trekvite møblane og skinn-salongen.

Bjørhei, Lomen *(side 55)*

Denne gamle, freda bygningen i Lomen, Valdres er også privat galleri for akvarell-målaren som bur her. Ho har vanlegvis veggane fulle av måleri, så det trengs ikkje så mykje ekstra dekor. I slike tilfelle er det spesielt viktig å få ei skikkeleg ramme på interiøret. Her har vi derfor måla golvlista og dørrammene mørke for å gje meir tyngde nederst. Langsetter taket har vi måla ein lett drue-ranke.

Valdres Gardsbryggeri, Volbu *(side 58-61)*

Valdres Gardsbryggeri er truleg det minste kommersielle bryggeriet i Noreg. I dette ombygde fjøset har det vorte både praktiske produksjonslokale og ein koseleg pub. Bryggekjelen er rett bak baren i det same rommet der serveringa finn stad.

Interiøret er prega av enkle materialar og kraftige, handlaga møblar. Eg har her brukt ein enkel, rustikk stil i varme jordfargar med figurar omkransa av rosemåling.

Lyskapellet *(side 62-65)*

Det såkalla lyskapellet er ein del av Beitostølen Helsesportsenter og vart oppført som eit minnesmerke over grunnleggaren Erling Stordal. Glasmåleriet som dominerer kapellet vart skapt av Ferdinand Finne kort tid før han gjekk bort.

Kraftige bjelkar formar ei stjerne som fyller det femkanta rommet frå hjørne til hjørne. Vi forgylte bjelkane med bladgull og måla ein lett drueranke oppå. Taket er mørk blått med stjerner i gull.

Bergo Hotell, Beitostølen *(side 66-67)*

Med enkle middel har vi her fått til ei koseleg kjellarstogo. Veggdekorasjonane er basert på historia om riddersprانget. Denne lokale legenda skildrar korleis ein riddar frå Valdres forelskar seg i ei jente frå ein rivaliserande familie i Gudbrandsdalen. Dei rømer saman, men blir forfølgde. Det siste panelet viser korleis dei slepp unna ved å hoppe over Ridderspranget, ei djup kløft på fjellet mellom Valdres og Gudbrandsdalen.

Fagernes Hotell *(side 68-71)*

På Fagernes Hotell har eg hatt dekorasjonsoppdrag fleire gonger. Matsalen har eit stilfullt, kontinentalt preg dominert av mørke tonar og messing. Her fekk vi bygd om himlinga for å skape skråpanel med store sjablongar i gull. I 'Klokkarstua' og 'Grillstuene' er det satsa på eit meir intimt preg med meir tilknytning til Valdres. Den såkalla 'blåsalen' er kanskje det mest karakteristiske rommet på hotellet, og etter mi meining eit av dei mest særprega og harmoniske interiøra eg har skapt.

Øystre Slidre Folkebibliotek *(side 72-73)*

Dette er eit av dei få store dekorasjonsoppdraga eg har hatt i offentlege bygg. I likheit med dei fleste andre bibliotek er det lite fri veggplass her, og interiøret er dominert av reolar med fargerike bokryggar. Vi bestemte oss for å utnytte den ledige veggplassen over hyllene og skape ein sjablongfris rundt heile rommet. Dette er mellom dei rikaste sjablongane eg har laga — opptil åtte forskjellige fargar vart trykte etter kvarandre.

Volbu Kyrkje *(side 74-75)*

Så lenge eg kan hugse har inngangen til Volbu kyrkje vore ganske grå og kjedeleg. Ein ny prest vi hadde for nokre år sidan ville gjerne gjera noko med dette. Han var redd det ville bli for komplisert dersom både prost og riksantikvar skulle innblandast, så han gjorde fort og greit undermålinga sjøl og fekk meg til å dekorere. Resultatet vart bra, så ingen har klaga på denne avgjerda.

Filefjellstuene *(side 76-77)*

Filefjellstuene er ein overnattingsplass og restaurant nær Tyin i Vang, etter hovedvegen mellom Oslo og Bergen. Med rik tilgang på gode råvarer, stor fagkunnskap og fantasi, har dei etter kvart fått seg eit namn som ein av dei mest interessante serveringsstadane i distriktet.

Valdres Vidaregåande Skule *(side 78-79)*

Denne salen i avdelinga for hotell- og næringsmiddelfag blir brukt både som kantine og i undervisninga for kokkefaglinja. Dei ville her gjerne ha eit rom med meir restaurant preg som ville gje studentar og tilsette ein meir inspirerande arbeidsplass.

Universitetet i Oslo *(side 80-85)*
Desse romma er kjellaretasjen i eit hybelhus i studentbyen på Sogn. Ein ynskte her å skapa eit festlokale inspirert av norsk tradisjon og bygdekultur. Med dette temaet sette vi i gang med å dekorere 'Valdresstuene' som desse romma no blir kalla. Den største utfordringa her var ein lang sal som tidlegare mest var brukt som lager. Her skapte vi ein 'riddersal' med middelalder-inspirert dekor og langbord som fyller heile salen.

Vesterland Hotel, Sogndal *(side 86)*
Dette 'meditasjonshuset' er ein del av Vesterland hotel nær Sogndal. I denne vesle bygningen finn du både boblebad og sauna i tillegg til dette meditasjonsrommet. Her har eg laga enkle, abstrakte dekorasjonar som på mange måtar har den same funksjonen som glasmåleri har i eit kapell.

Utladalen Naturhus, Øvre Årdal *(side 87)*
Denne låven ved inngangen til Utladalen fungerer på sommarstid som ein informasjonsportal for folk som finn vegen hit. Rundt i rommet er det mykje informasjon om området, medan endeveggen er tenkt som ein visuell introduksjon til denne dramatiske dalen.

Dekorativ kunst for vår tid *(side 88-91)*
Det er ikkje så mange moderne interiør der tradisjonell dekor og rosemåling er heilt passande. Eg har derfor i mange år vore oppteken av å vidareføre og gje nytt liv til folkekunsten. Opp gjennom åra har eg utvikla ei rekkje stilartar som er baserte på norske tradisjonar, men prøvd tilpassa moderne materialar, møblar og byggeskikk.

Eg har måla ein heil del studier på lerret, eit par av dei er viste her. Tanken med desse dekorasjonane var hovudsakleg at dei kunne reproduserast i stort format direkte på vegg, spesielt i offentlege bygg.

USA

Binkhaven, Wisconsin *(side 94-97)*
Når du kjem til dette feriehuset i Wisconsin er det lett å tru at du er i Noreg. Dei to stabbura, som her blir brukte som gjesterom, er faktisk bygde i Telemark og frakta over til USA i deler. Desse husa er rikt dekorerte, slik det gjerne var vanleg i Telemark. I hovedhuset har eg rosemåla himlinga og dekorert mange detaljar rundt om i huset.

Ann Sather, Chicago *(side 98-105)*
Ann Sather er ei kjede av 'svenske' restaurantar i Chicago. Eg fekk det første dekorasjons-oppdraget her via ein kjenning, og sidan det har eg vore over kvar gong ein ny restaurant eller cafe har opna.

Til den første restauranten laga eg dekorasjonar over temaet 'Nils Holgerssons vidunderlige reise'. Seinare har det vorte ikkje berre svenske tema, men også norske. På dei mindre cafeane har dekoren lite direkte skandinavisk tilknytning.

Vesterheim, Decorah, Iowa *(side 106-109)*
Vesterheim Norwegian-American Museum i Iowa er faktisk det største etniske museet i USA. Eg har hatt kontakt med museet gjennom mange år, særleg med organisering av kurs i rosemåling.

Då museet fekk ny administrasjons-bygning, vart eg gjeven oppdraget med å dekorere interiøra. Det var sjølvsagt interesse for å ha eit tydeleg norsk særpreg, så i forsamlingssalen brukte eg primstaven som utganspunkt. Kvart veggfelt representerer ein månad og illustrerer dei viktigaste merkedagane. Under felta er dei tilhøyrande primstav-symbola viste saman med utvalde rim knytta til merkedagane.

I korridoren som leier inn til dette rommet har eg måla folk i bunadar frå heile landet, med stiliserte landskap frå dei ulike distrikta i bakgrunnen.

日本語の概要

ノルウェーのインテリア

　ノルウェーでは豪華な宮殿や大聖堂、立派な荘園などはほとんど見られません。ノルウェーの建築は壮大さには欠けるもののこの国の持つ自然の美しさは人間の作り出したもっとも豪華な建築物とは比べ物にもなりません。

　広大な地域が松の木に覆われるこの国では木が建築の主な素材として使われているのはおどろくにあたりません。ノルウェーでは中世のころからログハウスが建てられています。

　ペイントされたインテリアはノルウェーとスウェーデンの典型的なインテリアの特徴です。ヨーロッパ国内のインテリアはたいてい豪華な美術工芸品や家具に満たされていましたがノルウェーのペイントされたインテリアはそのものがひとつの芸術とも言えます。建物、家具と家の内装を一体として見るこの国では異なった要素の相互関係、協調性が注意深くインテリアに考慮されています。

ペイントされた部屋

　一般家庭でのペイントの伝統は18世紀に始まりました。この時期はノルウェーの発展期、また経済成長期でもあり、地方に近代化と変化をもたらした時期でもあります。特に芸術的な表現法は色々な方面にもたらされ豪華に装飾された工芸品やインテリアは発展とともにもたらされた新しい富を表現する一つの方法となりました。色の要素を各部屋に持ち入れ、典型的なのは青で統一された部屋、黄色または赤で統一された部屋などで、違う色を部屋ごとに取り入れるというのはごく普通なことであり、インテリアがペイントされてないのは貧しい家庭だけでした。

　この新しいペイントされたインテリアの流行の中心となったのが同時期に発展したロー

ズマリングと呼ばれる装飾的なスタイルです。ローズマリングとはノルウェー語で「バラの絵」を意味します。ローズマリングの装飾スタイルはルネッサンス、ロココ、バロックや帝政時代の要素をヨーロッパ全土より取り入れ、地元の装飾の伝統とアーティスト個人のスタイルをデザインの手順に踏まえています。代表的な例はこの本の14、37、47と97ページに見られます。とても順応性のある装飾的なスタイルで、鉢や箱、椅子や戸棚、ベッドのフレームにいたる家具までローズマリングが可能で、時には家のすべての壁や天井などもローズマリングで飾られています。

　産業革命化が進む19世紀の終わりのヨーロッパで、ローズマリングはノルウェーで卓越した装飾芸術としての勢いを失い、20世紀の初期にはなくなってしまったものと思われました。近年、ローズマリングへの興味が一新されましたが、現在のノルウェーでは正式な技術訓練の場などなく、ローズマリングは個人の趣味として楽しまれています。

現代のスカンディナヴィアンインテリア

　20世紀のスカンディナヴィアの建築様式やデザインはほとんどのヨーロッパの国々と同じようモダニズムが主流となりました。装飾芸術要素は最小限にとデザインの基礎にまで削られ、デザインと製造の両方の面で固体主義から一様で協調性のあるものに重点が置かれ、コンクリート、アルミニウムやガラスなどのモダンなハイテク素材が重視されるようになり、「スカンディナヴィアンデザイン」と言えば機能性とスタイルの代名詞として世界で知られるようになりました。

　この意図的にに今までのものからかけ離れようとする動きはノルウェーの芸術、工芸の伝統に大きなインパクトを及ぼし、次の世代へ受け継がれていくはずの職人の技術が一世代で失われてしまいました。

　無駄がない控えめなモダニズムはモダンな趣味趣向になじみやすいとは言うもののノル

ウェーは個人の趣向や選択を重んじる国です
のでほとんどの人が機能性以上のものを自分
の家に望み、且つノルウェーの伝統と国の特
徴を保持したいと望んでいます。この本に載
っている作品は色とインテリアデコレーショ
ンへの一新された興味とその必要性を立証す
るものです。

モダンな世界の装飾スタイル

　この本は私が40年の間に手がけたインテ
リアの中の数限られた作品を紹介するもので
す。ほとんどがノルウェーでの作品ですが、
スウェーデン、フランス、アメリカでの作品
もあります。私のスタイルを要約するなら伝
統に習っているが必ずしもすべての作品が伝
統的なスタイルではないということです。オ
リジナルスタイルのノルウェーの装飾ペイン
トは200年以上も前にはじまり、その時代
のインテリアのために特別に創作されたのも
のです。昔の建築と今とではスタイルが変わ
るのは当たり前のことなので、現在の建物で
伝統のスタイルがすんなりと当てはまるもの
は非常に少ないのです。私が前々から感じて
いることは今の時代にみあった装飾スタイル
の必要性です。— 素材、家具、現代の建物
の特徴に合う何か。その何かを見出すためノ
ルウェーの装飾工芸に新しい息を吹き込み、
現代化することに私は大変な努力を費やして
います。

伝統を保つ

　私がインテリアのアイデアを考えるときに
特に気にかけていることは、部屋、建物にあ
ったテーマを見つけることです。それと共に
どういった雰囲気が必要なのか — 明るくオ
ープンな感じ、フォーマルでエレガントそれ
ともカジュアルな雰囲気？焦点は部屋のつ
くり、家具、色彩、モールディング、装飾品
にいたるすべてが調和するようにデザインを
創造することです。私のデザインの意図は歴
史的なインテリアのレプリカを作ることでは
ないので、特別な歴史的スタイルにこだわっ
ているわけではありません。重要なのはユー
ザーが住みやすく、心地よい環境を作り出す
ことです。モダンなライフスタイルに感化さ
れてクリエイティヴな解決法が生まれたりす
ることもあるし、時には伝統的なテクニック
を応用し、新しく素晴らしいデザインを生み
出すことも可能です。このアプローチだと伝
統的なスタイルの直接コピーよりもより伝統
的なスカンディナヴィアのインテリアの調和
感を捕らえられるように思います。

　私の仕事は個人からの依頼がほとんどで
す。この本にある代表的な作品は伝統的なフ
ァームハウスのインテリアからモダンホーム
まで、それにコテージが最初のセクション
"ホーム (Home)" で紹介されています。こ
の何年かで数々のレストラン、ホテルやオフ
ィスなどの商業インテリアをも手がけていま
す。それが次のセクション "ワーク (Work)"
で紹介されています。商業インテリアのよう
な違った環境だとたびたび新しいチャレンジ
に出会ったりします。見た目のよさ、バラン
スのよさを創造するのにはある程度の妥協が
必要となります。空調システム、照明それに
健康、保安、清掃、維持管理に対しても気を
使わなくてはいけません。皮肉なことにノル
ウェーの装飾工芸と伝統はノルウェーよりも
アメリカでの関心のほうが高く、私の伝統的
な装飾作品はアメリカでのほうが高い地位を
得ています。私はアイオワ州デコラ市のノル
ウェー・アメリカ美術館、ヴェスターハイム
と特に強いつながりをもっています。お互い
の協力の下に私たちはローズマリングのクラ
スをのべ40年ほど開いています。精選され
た私のアメリカでのスカンディナヴィアンス
タイルのインテリアが最後のセクション "ノ
ルウェーをアメリカに (Bringing Norway to
America)" で紹介されています。

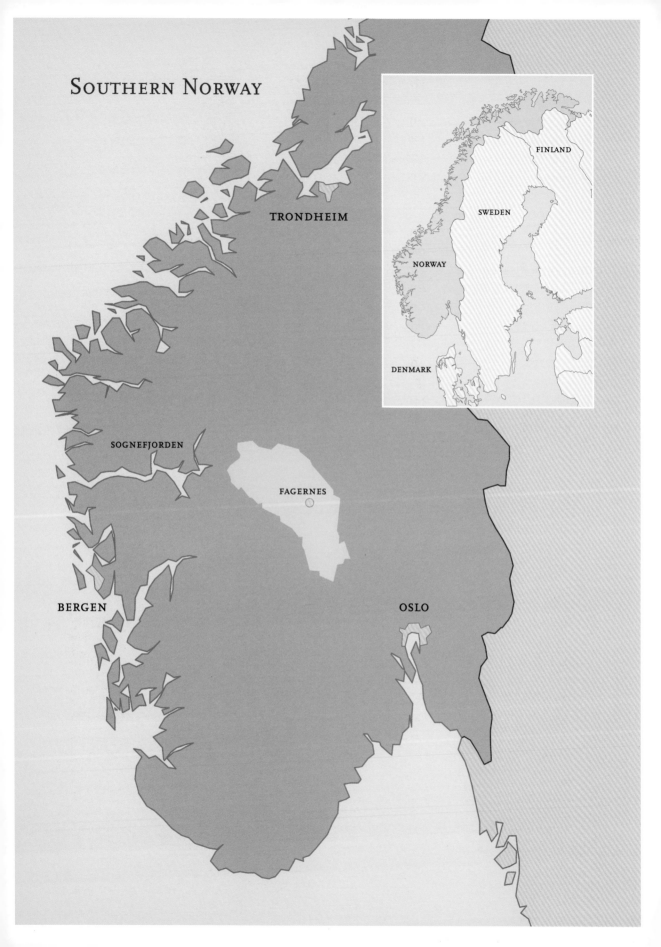

SOUTHERN NORWAY

TRONDHEIM

SOGNEFJORDEN

FAGERNES

BERGEN

OSLO

FINLAND

SWEDEN

NORWAY

DENMARK

ADDRESSES:

Valdres Gardsbryggeri
(pages 58-61)
N-2940 Heggenes
Norway
Tel: +47 61 34 04 95

Bergo Hotel
(pages 66-67)
N-2953 Beitostølen
Norway
Tel: +47 61 35 11 00
Fax: +47 61 35 11 01

Fagernes Hotel
(pages 68-71)
N-2900 Fagernes
Norway
Tel: +47 61 35 80 00
Fax: +47 61 35 80 01

Vesterland Hotel
(page 86)
N-6852 Sogndal
Norway
Tel: +47 57 62 71 00
Fax: +47 57 62 72 00

Utladalen Naturhus
(page 87)
N-6884 Øvre Årdal
Norway
Tel: +47 61 36 80 51/
+47 57 66 15 70

Filefjellstuene
(page 76-77)
N-2985 Tyinkrysset
Norway
Tel: +47 61 34 77 48
Fax: +47 613 67 848

U.S. ADDRESSES:

Ann Sather Restaurant
(pages 100-103)
929 West Belmont Ave
Chicago, IL 60657
Tel: 773-348-2378

Ann Sather Andersonville
(pages 98-99)
5207 North Clark St
Andersonville
Chicago, IL 60640
Tel: 773-271-6677

Ann Sather Cafe
(page 104)
3416 North Southport Ave
Chicago, IL 60657-1420
Tel: 773-404-4475

Ann Sather Cafe
(page 105)
3411 North Broadway St
Chicago, IL 60657-2904
Tel: 773-305-0024

Vesterheim Norwegian-American Museum
(pages 106-109)
523 West Water Street
P.O. Box 379
Decorah, IA 52101-0379
Tel: 563-382- 9681
Fax: 563-382-8828

I would like to thank:

First of all the Valdres newspaper, who awarded me their 100th anniversary culture price for the Valdres region in 2003. It was receiving this price that first made me think about creating a book about my interiors, and the prize money was put towards producing this book.

The department for culture in the district of Øystre Slidre where I live, who have supported the publication of this book.

All the people who have let us visit their homes, offices, restaurants and hotels in order to produce the photographs for this book. A particular thank to the Ann Sather restaurants of Chicago, Vesterheim; the Norwegian-American Museum in Decorah, Iowa and Dean E. Madden.

Everyone I have collaborated with over the years, including Knut Steinsrud, Heidi Fossheim, Sallie Haugen DeReus, Knut Øystein Bakken, Jan Arne Sebuødegård, my brother Kjell Arne and countless other painters, crafts people and carpenters.

Credits

The people who have helped create the interiors featured in this book:

Halldis Aarseth: 72-73,76-77
Ingebjørg Aarseth: 47-53, 55, 62-65, 76-77
Kjell Arne Aarseth: 47-49, 62-65, 80-85
Knut Øystein Bakken: 24-27, 32-41, 44-45, 66-67, 78-79, 100-101
Gro Bjørhei: 55
Sallie Haugen DeReus: 98-109
Inger Flaaten: 80-85
Heidi Fossheim: 42-45, 50-54, 62-65, 68-71
Darryl Henning: 106-109
Mary Lou: 98-99
Marilyn Madden: 106
Dean E. Madden: 94-97
Mary Parker: 98-101
Jan Arne Sebuødegård: 70, 80-85
Hallvard Skattebu: 40-41
Norma Wangsnes: 106
Anne Åsen: 30-31

Photo courtesy of Karen Hoyt

Sigmund (right) takes a break with restaurant owner Tom Tunney and collaborator Sallie Haugen DeReus after decorating a new Ann Sather cafe in Chicago in April 2004.

Photos courtesy of Tor Harald Skogheim

Øystre Slidre Kommune
(The District of Øystre Slidre)

Øystre Slidre is a community of about 3100 inhabitants, bordering on the mountainous Jotunheimen national park in the northern part of the Valdres valley.

The primary sources of income here are agriculture and tourism, there are numerous opportunities for sports and outdoor pursuits all year round. Every winter a network of cross-country skiing tracks is prepared, while the thriving ski resort of Beitostølen caters for other winter sports.

Øystre Slidre Kommune has a rich and vital cultural scene where local crafts, music and singing traditions are maintained. We are lucky in that many artists have chosen to settle in the district, Sigmund Aarseth being one of them. In 2000 we commissioned him to decorate the district's official Millennium site—our new library (featured on pages 72-73). He completed this commission in an outstanding manner that everyone in the area greatly appreciates!

By offering our support to the publication of this book the District Council of Øystre Slidre wishes to show its appreciation for the work Sigmund has done and continues to do to advance and maintain the cultural heritage of our district.

Anne S. Moen
Head of Culture, Øystre Slidre District Council

VALDRES
the local newspaper for the district of Valdres

Our local newspaper 'Valdres' could last year look back on 100 years in the service of our valley. The first ordinary edition appeared on April 7th 1903. The newspaper developed fast, and after two months the circulation was already 1400 copies. To date 'Valdres' has maintained a strong position in the valley with nearly 10.000 subscribers, including many outside our own district and even abroad.

Every year since 1964 'Valdres' has been awarding a price for outstanding cultural efforts. Many societies, artists and others working in the cultural sector have through the years been given the honor of this award.

When the newspaper celebrated its centennial in 2003, we chose to give a special 100th anniversary award. On this occasion it was natural to honor the artist and promoter of local culture, Sigmund Aarseth in Volbu. His work has been appreciated both in Valdres and the United States.

Aarseth was awarded the prize for his achievements in disseminating the culture of Valdres in Norway as well as abroad. He is — and will continue to be — a major contributor to making Valdres known. This is an effort we highly appreciate.

Torbjørn Moen
Editor of 'Valdres'

ORDER FORM

To order more copies of this book, or Sigmund's previous book, *'Aarseth's Rosemaling Design; Norwegian Rosemaling Telemark Style',* fill in this order form and mail or fax it to:

Nordic Arts
3208 Snowbrush Place,
Fort Collins, CO 80521
Fax (970) 229-5683   Phone (970) 229-9846

Or email your order to: **Diaedwards@cs.com**

Name:

Address:

City: *State:*   *Zip:*

Telephone:

Email:

Painted Rooms; Scandinavian Interiors by Sigmund Aarseth:

☐ copies at **$34.95** each $_____

Aarseth's Rosemaling Design; Norwegian Rosemaling Telemark Style:

☐ copies at **$29.95** each $_____

Sub total $_____

For orders from within Colorado, please add 3% sales tax: $_____
Shipping and handling: for orders within the United States,
please add $5 for the first book and $2 for each extra added book: $_____
For deliveries outside the United States, please enquire for current postage rates.

Sale Total $_____

....

❑ I have enclosed a check for the sale total
❑ I have supplied my credit card details below: **VISA** **MasterCard** **DISCOVER** NOVUS

Type of card: ❑ Visa ❑ MasterCard ❑ Discover

Name on card:

Card No: Expiration date: